Landships
British Tanks in the First Wo[rld War]

Frontispiece: A heavy armoured hull running on narrow tyres was unsuitable on the shelled and waterlogged ground of the Western Front. This Rolls-Royce lies abandoned on the 'road' near Arras in 1917. Its thin armour has been supplemented by a cladding of Uralite.

Landships
British Tanks in the First World War

David Fletcher

LONDON HER MAJESTY'S STATIONERY OFFICE

© *Crown copyright 1984*
First published 1984

ISBN 0 11 290409 2

Cover: A Mark V male tank of 2nd Battalion, Tank Corps, moving up for the Battle of Amiens, 8 August 1918.

Contents

Introduction 1
Chapter I 1915, Year of Experiment 3
Chapter II 1916, The First Tanks 14
Chapter III 1917, Expansion and Fulfilment 21
Chapter IV 1918, Year of Victory 31
Chapter V 1919, Curtain Call 45

Introduction

Unfortunate as it may be, warfare sometimes brings out the best in people. It will tap hidden veins of courage or provoke flights of inventive genius that remain dormant in peacetime. At no time was this more striking than in the First World War and in no sphere more dramatic than that of land warfare. The main belligerents were all highly industrialised, even before war broke out, and this mechanical energy was bent to the cause on a scale that would never have been imagined at the turn of the century.

Although, for the purpose of this book, we are studying events in Britain, it would be inaccurate to imply that this was the only country seeking a mechanical solution to trench warfare. In France, Germany and the United States similar machines reached the production stage, while limited development took place in Italy and Russia. However, there is no doubt that Britain and France led the field in terms of effort applied and official backing, and that the British went furthest in developing a mechanical solution and first employed it in battle. It was Britain, too, which christened it with the name by which it is still best recognized worldwide and, perhaps typically, this name has nothing whatever to do with what the thing does; we call it the tank

Put simply the tank is a device which transports men and guns, behind the relative safety of armour plate, to a point on the battlefield where they can do most good, or harm. Since the component parts — the guns, armour, power unit and tracks — are integral, then the whole thing becomes a weapon in itself, rather than a means of transport for a weapon.

The idea of armouring self-propelled vehicles for war is nearly as old as the first such vehicles. An advertisement which appeared in 1855, towards the end of the Crimean War, showed James Cowen's concept of an armed and armoured steam traction engine which, like Bodicea's mythical chariot, also sprouted scythes for cutting down enemy troops. Its effectiveness was never put to the test since the Government refused to associate itself with such a barbaric project. The apparent success of the Royal Engineer's traction engines in the Boer War encouraged Lord Roberts to place an order for an armoured version pulling a string of armoured wagons, a road-bound version of the armoured railway trains then in use. These road trains started to arrive in South Africa in 1900 but none of them was ever employed as intended. Then, in 1902, Frederick Simms, a British motoring pioneer, demonstrated a large war-car of his own design at the Crystal Palace. Unlike the bulky steamers, it was powered by an internal combustion engine, which being more compact, allowed the designer greater flexibility. The War Office chose to ignore it.

In the years leading up to the First World War a variety of armoured cars appeared all over Europe. Since each was developed in isolation, often at the behest of a particular engineer or industrialist, there was no such thing as progressive design and many of them were of questionable military value. Such trends as there were emphasized protection, at the expense of fire-power and mobility, so it is interesting to note that one of the few designed by a soldier, Captain Genty of the French Army, consisted simply of a large machine-gun mounted on an open car. Protection thus lay in speed and manoeuvrability, rather than armour plate. The degree of priority to accord these various factors has exercised the designers of fighting vehicles ever since.

The outbreak of war in August 1914 led to the use of armoured cars on a large scale. The exposed flank of the invading German Army, as it swung through Belgium, invited hit-and-run tactics for which high-powered touring cars were ideal. The Belgians took to the idea with gusto and they were soon joined by members of the Eastchurch Squadron, Royal Naval Air Service, under Commander C. R. Samson RN. The Squadron supplemented its aerial activities with raids against enemy cavalry patrols by road. Samson's men attracted the attention of their superiors, who sanctioned development of bigger and better armoured cars until, by the spring of 1915, some seventy armoured cars and lorries were operating in support of Allied forces in Flanders. Success was limited by the need for these converted civilian vehicles to keep to the roads; carrying weight far in excess of their designed capabilities, they were useless across country. Once the battle lines were established and the trenches dug, opportunities for mobile action were almost non-existent. The armoured cars were then transferred to other theatres of war where these restrictive conditions did not apply and later they were handed over to the Army.

All that remained in France was a void, and an idea. Among those who had found their outlet in the new kind of fighting were a few inventive souls who sought to adapt the principle to the new conditions. Since these men sprang from the ranks of the Royal Naval Air Service, it was almost by default that the initial responsibility for designing the tank came from this quarter. It led in time to the formation of a special experimental unit, No. 20 Squadron RNAS, which was established, not without some Admiralty opposition, in the relatively uncongenial surroundings of Wormwood Scrubs, London, while the War Office, with one notable exception, looked defiantly the other way.

The First Lord of the Admiralty was Winston Churchill, a man whose vision was never bounded by departmental limitations, and he acted as the initial catalyst to get things moving. His most positive contribution was the setting up of the Landships Committee early in 1915. This body, which, in due course, became a joint services organization, began its deliberations by deciding, amidst a deluge of well-meant advice, between the respective merits of machines running on enormous wheels or caterpillar tracks. It was soon realized that the latter were best suited to the circumstances so the next step was to evaluate the various types then available.

The home of the caterpillar track in 1915 was the United States. The vast scale and variety of its agricultural industry provided the perfect breeding ground for invention and some dozen or more firms were building and selling tracklayers to the world market. Thus it came about that the Landships Committee, through its most venerable member, Colonel R. E. B. Crompton, began to import a variety of commercial tractors for evaluation, while this grand old Victorian engineer began designing landships to suit them. Crompton's deliberations, valuable as they were, soon tried the patience of the Committee's dynamic secretary, Albert Stern. This remarkable young man, who substituted an iron will for technical acumen, transferred the main stream of research into the hands of two other men with the ability to see the project through swiftly. They may justly be called the fathers of the tank.

Lieutenant Walter Wilson was an engineer of undoubted genius; his partner, William Tritton, was the managing director of a Lincoln-based firm of agricultural engineers, William Foster and Co. Ltd. Between them they had the facility for invention and the propensity for action which bore fruit in a remarkably short space of time, bearing in mind the revolutionary nature of their task. It is no surprise that, from a small army of claimants, the Royal Commission on Awards to Inventors, which sat in 1919, adjudged their contribution worthy of the highest award.

It soon became clear that no matter how suited they were to agriculture, none of the American tractors really had the stamina required for an armoured fighting vehicle. The crude tracks, despite their sprung rollers, would not accept the weight of an armoured superstructure, so, in due course, Tritton scrapped the idea and developed an entirely new track of his own design. With hindsight it is clear that this was the masterstroke. In one move, he discovered the ideal means to support the weight of the vehicle and thereby freed himself from the limitations imposed by a commercial system intended for a totally different purpose. It is no exaggeration to claim that this was the feature, above all others, that made the British tank the outstanding success that it was. With the notable exception of the little French Renault, all the overseas designs were relative failures because they incorporated the basic Holt tractor suspension and track, which meant that the tank was designed to suit an existing chassis instead of the other way round.

Tritton and Wilson exploited their freedom from existing commercial systems to the full. They carried the track right around the extremities of the hull in order to provide maximum cross-country performance and trench-crossing potential. Thus was born the familiar rhomboid shape which today is regarded as the trademark of the early tank.

The original concept that gave rise to the tank was that of the siege engine. It was to be a particular device for a particular job, the safe crossing of no-man's-land, secure from the hail of machine-gun bullets. The tangle of barbed wire would be torn down, the trenches crossed and the stalemate ended. Indeed, so limited was this original idea that the tank was seen as expendable, as something to be abandoned once the siege was broken, leaving the army free to resume its traditional mobility with traditional arms. In the event both practice and experience conspired to alter this. In practice crews always tried to bring their charges home once the job was done, while experience taught that the duties of the tank did not end once the trenches were crossed. Far from being a simple mechanical battering-ram the tank proved to be the ideal means to exploit military advantage and so, despite many vicissitudes, it gradually became the ultimate manifestation of mobile land warfare in the machine age. As the war progressed, the tanks were improved and their variety increased to suit the new-found role while new tactics were painfully evolved for their employment. Notwithstanding their complexities, modern tanks are still a balanced combination of the basic features first embodied in 'Mother' back in 1915.

The following pages tell the story of the British tank in the First World War with the help of original photographs. The principal aim is to record the development of the weapon as a machine, from the primitive tractors of 1915 to the sophisticated giants of 1918, against the background of the battles in which they fought. The pictures show the tank at some of the high points in its career; at Flers and Arras, Cambrai and Amiens. They show it in life and death, in Flanders mud and desert sand, while behind and around it we see the horrifying, devastated landscape in which it moved. Above all we see the men whom it destroyed or preserved and, in their haunted faces, the tragedy of a war in which the tank first became an instrument of victory.

Finally the reader is invited to supplement this experience with a visit to the Tank Museum, at Bovington Camp in Dorset, where some ten examples of First World War tanks are on display, along with their ancillary equipment and the ephemera of the men who worked and fought with them.

CHAPTER I
1915, Year of Experiment

Contrary to popular belief, the caterpillar, or crawler, track was not invented for tanks. Indeed unconsummated patents can be traced back to the eighteenth century and a variety of practical tracked vehicles was available, mostly in the United States, from the early years of the twentieth century. They were designed for service in the farming and logging industries, starting with enormous steam-powered models for clearing swamp lands, and developed into a range of petrol-engined types of various sizes. The first military application dates from 1907, when a large machine was tested by the British Army. It was built by a Grantham firm, Richard Hornsby and Sons, to the design of their managing director, David Roberts. This resulted, in 1909, in the production of a second model, powered by a six-cylinder paraffin engine, which was tested by the Royal Artillery as a gun tractor. To the gunners, proud of their matched teams of horses, the appearance of this noisy, smelly contraption was little short of heresy and the opposition was overwhelming. This virtually ended Hornsbys' part in tracked-vehicle development and they sold off their patents to the Holt Company in California. Holt's tracklaying system was probably superior to the British design; it was certainly simpler, so it is believed that the American company were more interested in Robert's transmission system than his tracks.

Although tracks were superior to wheels for movement over broken ground, it would seem that the military regarded them mainly as a method of hauling heavy artillery and other loads. It took a few dedicated individuals to appreciate how the system could be adapted to warfare in a more direct sense. In Britain, Captain T. G. Tulloch, looking at the Hornsby tractor, imagined how effective it could be if a large metal box (a 'tank', he prophetically called it) was fitted to carry soldiers into action. In 1911 an Austrian, Gunther Burstyn, designed what was, in effect a tank, which was turned down successively by the Austrian and German Governments. A year later, Lancelot de Mole, an inventive Australian, offered the British War Office his design for an armoured tracklayer but it met with an equally apathetic response. The designs were so far ahead of their time that nobody appreciated the need for them; they were quietly pigeon-holed and forgotten.

The twelve years that separate the demonstration of Simm's War Car and Commander Samson's activities in Belgium were lean years for the development of British armoured-cars. The two or three cars that were built played no part in later events and, indeed, were never taken up by the Army. The War Office was only interested in mechanization with regard to supply and transportation, as the motor lorry began to replace the horse-drawn wagon. Yet the period between September and December 1914 saw great strides initiated by the Admiralty. From Samson's early, improvised design stemmed a line of armoured cars which, by the end of the year, culminated in the classic, turreted Rolls-Royce. These were supplemented by armoured lorries mounting larger guns and by a couple of armoured bus chassis which served as troop carriers. All of this development came to an end, at least in Europe, when the trench lines were established.

The problems of trench warfare had been foreseen as long ago as the American Civil War but no effective tactics had been formulated to deal with them. Conventional military thinking on all sides tended to see no further than an escalation of traditional weapons, notably artillery; it required people with an objective view and an inventive turn of mind to imagine an unconventional solution to the problem and it was Britain's good fortune to have such men placed where they could do some good. Among these, two stand out as initiators of the tank idea. One was Colonel Ernest Swinton, the British Army's official war correspondent in France; the other was Winston Churchill, First Lord of the Admiralty. Each pondered and wrote, entreated and cajoled, according to his status, until things began to move. Swinton had the advantage, for a soldier, of being at the front without any direct responsibilities of command. Thus he was able to appreciate the nature of the war from a detached viewpoint. His ideas crystallized around a report he had obtained about a Holt tractor that had been demonstrated near Antwerp. The type was, even then, being adopted by the Royal Artillery as a prime mover for heavy guns and Swinton felt that its cross-country ability could be put to better use in crossing the broken ground between the trenches and tearing up the wire. He laid his scheme before the War Office, where it met with a lukewarm reception. Churchill, on the other hand, had more immediate success. The armoured car squadrons, by their very nature, had attracted a breed of men, familiar with mechanical devices, who found their desire for action satisfied by the piratical activities of these units. Deprived of the opportunity in France, they either took their cars to other theatres or looked for new ways of adapting them to the present circumstances.

Some of the schemes devised by these men were already in the air before the end of 1914 and these gradually percolated through the channels of the Admiralty Air Department until they came to the attention of the First Lord, who was not without ideas of his own. One of these, which appealed to Churchill immensely, was to crush the enemy trenches flat by means of steam rollers, preferably two of them, harnessed together. The Director of the Air Department, Commodore Murray Sueter, was directed to act upon the First Lord's suggestion, so two road rollers were borrowed for experiments at Wormwood Scrubs. It was soon discovered that steam rollers do not like working in pairs and, further, that their smooth rolls prevent them from operating at all on soft ground. Drawn, however unwillingly, into the project, Sueter set some of his staff to work on alternative schemes. A few years earlier he had advised Captain Scott to take some light caterpillar tractors to Antarctica and, recalling these, he decided to examine the present availability of tracklayers in Britain. In fact there was only one firm making them, the Pedrail Transport Company of Fulham, which was presided over by the strange and cantankerous figure of Bramah J. Diplock. He was a road haulage expert who, for the last eighteen years, had been developing, and attempting to market, a complicated transport system for the colonies. His ingenious but impractical invention, the Pedrail, was a particularly free-running tracklaying system but it was impossible to steer in the usual way since each vehicle ran on a single, full-width track. For this reason it was only sold as a light, horse-drawn cart, for use in quarries and on farms, but at least it would serve as an example. Sueter had a cart brought round to Horse Guards Parade, where he and Churchill pushed it around for a while until the latter was convinced that it held more promise than his idea of using steam rollers. Two of the little Pedrail wagons were purchased and despatched to Wormwood Scrubs, where one of them later formed the basis of a manually propelled infantry shield. This was one of the oldest ideas in warfare, brought up to date in terms of materials and the addition of the track. A full-size wooden mock-up was built and mounted on the Pedrail unit by the Royal Naval Air Service and there was even talk of fitting it with a motorcycle engine. In the event, however, the project was taken no further in Britain.

Meanwhile the Army had been active. In order to examine Swinton's proposals, a demonstration was arranged at Aldershot for senior War Office officials to study a Holt caterpillar tractor. The machine they saw was one that had recently arrived from America for the Royal Artillery. It was powered by a 75hp petrol engine and ran on two lightly sprung track bogies at the rear and a single steering roller at the front. The short track base, compared with the length of the tractor, limited its cross-country ability but it was sturdy and reliable and, what is more, obviously capable of further development. The War Office established a committee of senior officers to take the matter forward and, in February 1915, the day after Sueter's Horse Guards demonstration, a Holt was tested at Shoeburyness. In an effort to reproduce conditions in France, trenches were dug and some wire laid out. However, in the absence of suitable armour plate, a heavily loaded trailer was attached to the rear of the machine to represent the extra weight. Even the weather was against it, for rain had turned the ground into a swamp and the trial was as unscientific as can be imagined. Although the tractor managed to cross the trench, the trailer became stuck and the tow-bar sheared, at which point the War Office committee became discouraged and set off for home. In their view the project was dead already.

It is at this point that there emerges perhaps the saddest figure among those who became involved with the tank, Colonel Rookes Evelyn Bell Crompton. Then in his seventies, he had seen brief service as a boy in the trenches before Sebastopol during the Crimean War and had latterly made a name for himself as an expert in mechanical traction and electricity. His experience of mechanical traction dated from his years in India with the Rifle Brigade in the 1860s, when he had been responsible for the introduction of long-distance road steamers for the Indian Government. During the Boer War he had commanded a volunteer unit of electrical engineers who had also operated steam engines. In private life, he had founded a successful business supplying domestic electricity. A tall stooping figure, the epitome of the Victorian engineer of many parts, he was already bombarding the War Office with advice when the war began. His ideas were all eminently sensible but his desire for perfection conflicted with the urgency of wartime work. In February 1915 he submitted what he called his 'trench straddling machine', which was a species of giant tractor with a special deck to carry troops behind armour. It was intended to run across no-man's-land and pause astride the enemy trench while the troops came down through a trapdoor to deal with the opposition. The War Office rejected the scheme at once but Crompton was invited to join an Admiralty team, called the Landships Committee, which met for the first time on 22 February 1915.

The active figurehead of this body was Eustace Tennyson D'Eyncourt, the Director of Naval Construction. Crompton was retained as technical adviser on account of his reputation and the other members were mostly RNAS officers appointed by Sueter for their enthusiasm and varied expertise. The main object of their initial discussions was the choice between caterpillar tracks or very large wheels as the ideal means of cross-country transport. The theory behind large-wheeled vehicles harks back to one of the earliest projects put forward by an RNAS officer as a means of winning the war. Flight-Commander Hetherington was blessed with an imagination that H. G. Wells would have appreciated: he visualised an enormous machine, 30m (100ft) long, 24m (80ft) wide, and 14m (46ft) high, running on three 12m (40ft) diameter wheels. This was no trench-crossing machine, no siege breaker; it was a true leviathan capable of crushing all in its path, of fording the Rhine and driving straight into Germany. It was also a totally impossible idea, far beyond the capabilities of contemporary engineering and, in the cold light of day, it was quickly passed over.

Even so, the idea of the 'Big Wheel' remained, in a reduced form, and would reappear shortly. Meanwhile Commodore Sueter had been at work on a design of his own. Impressed with the potential of the Pedrail track, he approached Diplock with an idea for a tracked landship running on a parallel pair of tracks. Diplock replied that his system could not be made to operate in this way and suggested instead a pair of track units in tandem, like the bogies of a railway carriage, which could be driven and steered in either direction. Draughtsmen at the Pedrail works drew up Sueter's design, which, with its central conning tower and nautical helm, looked rather like a submarine on tracks. This was no coincidence, for Sueter, in earlier years, had been associated with the design of the first Royal Navy submarines and was using some of those techniques on his landship project.

Crompton, meanwhile, had been trying, without much success, to obtain details of the battle front from the War Office in order to perfect his own designs. From his Kensington home he began to issue a whole series of drawings, the first of which looked like a very long shed on tracks. Like Sueter, he employed the Pedrail track system but by contrast the Colonel was designing troop carriers to move trench-storming parties across the killing ground between the opposing trenches. At the same time he was attending committee meetings and touring the country, interviewing potential contractors and examining likely products. Tireless and dedicated, despite his years, Crompton was going to do the whole thing himself if he could.

By the end of March another wheeled design was on offer, also from Crompton. Despite an apparent preference for tracks, he was worried that they would get tangled up in barbed wire and, in any case, he was finding Diplock an impossible man to deal with. His new design, known as the 'Big Wheel' machine, was an articulated troop-carrier running on four 4·5m (15ft) diameter wheels of the traction-engine type. The leading element contained the power unit, drive train and crew, while the rear section provided accommodation for seventy troops. Models of

1 A 75hp Holt tractor in Army service at Gaza. Widely exported before the war, this vehicle was one of the primary sources of inspiration for tank inventors in at least four countries. In Britain alone it played no direct part in the mechanical development of the tank.

Crompton's two designs were shown to the Landships Committee and, at Churchill's instigation, contracts were placed for six of each; the tracklayers with Foden and the 'Big Wheel' with Fosters of Lincoln.

Lieutenant Walter Wilson RNVR was, at this time, based in Huntingdon, supervising construction of a fleet of armoured lorries for the RNAS. He was a gifted engineer who had left the Royal Navy after a brief career, to become a pioneer designer of motor-cars. His Wilson-Pilcher of 1902, although hardly a stirring commercial success, featured a four-speed pre-selector gearbox and horizontal engine. At the outbreak of war he had been working for the Hallford lorry firm in Kent and had only returned to the Navy early in 1915. In April he was instructed to go to Lincoln, where he would meet William Tritton and, with him, examine a wooden mock-up of the 'Big Wheel' machine, which was taking shape at Foster's works. Like Crompton, Tritton was convinced that tracks would prove unsuitable. His own firm had built the Centipede tracklayer in 1912 and it had been a dismal commercial failure. Since then Fosters had been awarded a valuable contract by the Admiralty to build a fleet of wheeled, petrol tractors for the Royal Marine artillery, powered by a six-cylinder Daimler engine, and mechanical components from these were to be incorporated into the 'Big Wheel' design. Looking at the huge wooden replica, the two men realized that it would not work. Besides the great height, which would make it a prime target for enemy guns, the pressure exerted by the four giant wheels would immobilize it on soft ground and, if it broke down on the way to the front, the sort of traffic jam it might cause defied description. Tritton therefore prepared drawings for a lighter version that would take its power from a mobile generator, stationed behind the lines, since it relied on electric traction. However, this idea was rejected, too, because a break in the cable could leave it stranded on the battlefield, to be reduced by the enemy at their leisure.

One problem common to all the designers was a continuing lack of knowledge of conditions at the front. In an effort to remedy this, Colonel Crompton, along with Hetherington and Stern, set out for France to see for themselves. They spent the night at Dunkirk and then proceeded next day as far as St Omer, where a staff officer abruptly turned them round, since they had no official clearance to enter the fighting zone. Predictably this annoyed the elderly Crompton, who was still suffering the after-effects of a sleepless night due to the constant coming and going of aircraft over his hotel. However, the views he had of narrow village streets and bridges convinced him that

2 Designed to haul heavy artillery for the Royal Navy, these big tractors made two contributions to the story of the tank. Their builders, William Foster and Co. of Lincoln, became the first firm to build tanks in Britain and their six-cylinder Daimler engine with its transmission system, was employed in all tanks Marks I to IV.

his long landship would never get to the front in one piece, so when he got home he redesigned it in an articulated form. He saw this as having a further advantage in the event of one end getting stuck in a shell hole, for in that case the other half would be able to pull it out again.

Progress was painfully slow and, in an attempt to get things moving, Commodore Sueter permitted another of his officers to begin a rival project of his own. This was Lieutenant MacFie, whom Sueter described as a 'caterpillar expert'. MacFie had first attended the Landships Committee meetings in this capacity on the strength of a suggestion he placed before his superior officer regarding caterpillar gun tractors; now he was to have the chance to design a tank. He was provided with funds, and the chassis of an Alldays and Onions three-ton lorry from the naval pool, which he took to the works of Nesfield and McKenzie in Ealing. He and Nesfield were to co-operate on the design, but their story may be quickly told. The design was prepared and a model built, but the two partners soon fell out and successively kidnapped the little model to reinforce their independent claims to its design. The full-size prototype languished in a half-completed state for some months before the project was closed down altogether. Although neither man claimed to have solved the track problem itself, the design displayed one peculiarity, a well-angled track for climbing, which was a feature of the ultimately successful Tritton design. There is no reason to suppose that Tritton or Wilson drew any inspiration from the Nesfield/MacFie model yet both protagonists in this undignified squabble gained a small reward after the war.

By the end of April it seems that all, except perhaps Tritton, were convinced that tracks were the answer. Diplock's Pedrail was out of favour so it was necessary to find an alternative. With Sueter's approval, Crompton sent an associate, George Field, to the United States with instructions to examine the various machines available there. In the meantime there were others to be seen nearer home. One was the Killen-Strait, a tiny agricultural tractor built in Wisconsin, which ran on three sets of tracks like a tricycle. The other was a type similar to the Holt, called the Bullock Creeping Grip Tractor, which was made in Chicago. The Killen-Strait was delivered to Wormwood Scrubs, where it was examined by Colonel Crompton on 27 April while the next day the Colonel, accompanied by Hetherington and Wilson, went to inspect a Bullock tractor working on the Greenhithe marshes near Dartford. The result of these examinations was interesting: the Killen-Strait remained with 20 Squadron at Wormwood Scrubs, where it later played an important role as a demonstrator; the Bullock tracks appeared to Crompton more suited to immediate development, so he redrew his landship to incorporate them

3 The little Killen-Strait tractor during a demonstration at Wormwood Scrubs. Circus tricks such as this proved to be a useful way of illustrating the caterpillar idea to important visitors, including Winston Churchill and Lloyd George.

and encouraged the Admiralty to order a pair of these machines from America.

On 7 May 1915, the contracts for the 'Big Wheel' and Pedrail Machines were reduced to one of each. It did not matter very much since the former was already discredited and, because of industrial trouble at Fodens, work on the latter had been transferred to another contractor. Thus the Pedrail Machine went through a short but troubled gestation period as it was overtaken by events and passed from hand to hand, still incomplete, before finally coming to rest at Bath. Here, at the works of Stothert and Pitt, it was ultimately completed in unarmoured form for the Trench Warfare Department, which planned to employ it as a mobile flamethrower. It underwent trials at their establishment at Porton Down on Salisbury Plain but, despite putting up a good performance, it was never adopted for service. In fact, it was a most interesting design, which looked, at first sight, like nothing so much as a single-deck tramcar running on tracks. Each Pedrail bogie supported its own power unit, a six-cylinder Aster engine, and transmission. It could be driven from either end but it required a good deal of space in which to turn and was very limited in its trench-crossing ability by the short tracks. It could, however, manage a top speed of 24kmph (15mph)

4 The completed Pedrail Landship during trials on Porton Down. The arrangement of the tandem track units is clearly seen, but the armoured body was never fitted.

despite a weight of 32 tons. There was a plan, produced later in the war, to adapt the chassis as a road-making machine, since it had been noted that the stamping action of the tanks tended to consolidate, rather than tear up, the road surface. Although this was never done, it did lead, in 1918, to the production of a prototype Pedrail lorry called the Roller Track Wagon.

For Tritton, the abandonment of the 'Big Wheel' project meant the loss of lucrative war work to his firm so, in order to keep Foster's name in the running, he became involved in another rather outlandish plan. This had its origins in the early trials of the prototype Foster-Daimler tractor. The order for these tractors stemmed from a scheme initiated by Admiral Sir Reginald Bacon of the Coventry Ordnance Works in Glasgow. Bacon had approached the First Lord with an offer to build heavy howitzers for the Royal Marines but Churchill would only accept them on condition that a suitable means of transportation could be provided to go with them. The big Foster-Daimler was built especially for this work, although, in due course, it proved useful for all kinds of things. Attending the initial trials with Tritton, the Admiral watched the tractor negotiating a special, portable bridge and both men realized that if the tractor could be made to carry and lay a bridge of its own, the trench-crossing problem could be solved. A design was worked out at Lincoln and official approval obtained for production of a trial machine based on one of the tractors. It is not possible now to apportion credit for the design but, in April 1915,

Bacon was given command of the Dover Patrol and the machine has always been known as the Tritton Trench Crosser.

One of the tractors was duly modified; the front axle was removed and extended frames added to the front, containing a pair of wheels in tandem. Two portable girders were slung ahead of the rear wheels and attached to the tractor with chains so that the procedure for crossing a trench was as follows. The machine would approach the trench and push its nose across until a skid on the forward end rested on the far side. The girders, which served as a bridge for the hind wheels, were then released to fall across the trench. Once the tractor had reached the other side, it dragged the bridging girders on to flat ground and reversed over them again so that they could be lifted back into place, whereupon the vehicle was ready to proceed. The idea was simple. On 11 May the tractor arrived at Shoeburyness for trials over the special test course and at once the first snag in the design became obvious. It crossed the first trench successfully but there were two of them and, since the machine needed a clear space of 7·6m (25ft), in which to recover the bridge, it was stranded. Subsequently it tried to cross both trenches without the aid of the girders and became so firmly stuck that it had to be hauled out by a Holt tractor that was standing by. Although it was mentioned in the report, nobody seems to have paid any heed to the fact that during this rescue operation the Holt successfully crossed both trenches! Drawings had been prepared for an armoured version of the Tritton Trench Crosser but with the failure of these trials the project was dropped.

Early June saw the 'Big Wheel' project finally abandoned, which implied that tracks of one sort or another would be the best answer. It also saw the return of Colonel Swinton. Despite the poor response to his earlier approaches, he had found an ally in Lieutenant-Colonel Maurice Hankey, Secretary to the Committee of Imperial Defence. In an effort to keep his project alive, Swinton had prepared a paper for British Headquarters in France entitled 'The necessity for Machine-Gun Destroyers', in which he visualized armed and armoured tractors emerging from pits behind the British line to lead the infantry and subdue the machine-guns. He mentioned caterpillars and an automatic two-pounder gun but, it seems clear, he had no specific design in mind. His paper caused a stir and invited some rebukes from above but it had the beneficial effect of putting him in touch with the Landships Committee, which, at the end of June, was expanded to include War Office representatives.

Whether it was Swinton's suggestion or a case of natural progression is not clear but, at the beginning of June, Colonel Crompton was instructed to drop his troop-carrier project in favour of turreted fighting machines with guns. On 14 June, the two Bullock tractors arrived at Liverpool and were delivered to the McEwan and Pratt works at

5 *The Tritton Trench Crosser was converted from a Foster-Daimler tractor. It was an early attempt to adapt a wheeled vehicle for the battlefield. William Tritton stands, hands on hips, alongside two officers.*

Burton-on-Trent. The Colonel had them joined with a flexible coupling of his own design to test his theories on articulation but the results of the trials were disappointing; it seemed impossible to get the two tractors to work in concert over trenches or shell holes. This project was also abandoned and shortly afterwards one of the machines was fitted with a most unlikely-looking arrangement of swinging wooden poles called 'Elephant's Feet', with which it was supposed to walk across trenches. This experiment was no more effective but the tracks were still the best available, so Field was ordered to purchase two extra-long sets from Chicago. In passing, it is interesting to note that in spite of the close secrecy that surrounded the entire landships project, the McEwan and Pratt works were overlooked by a large brewery and in easy sight from the Midland Railway main line to Derby. Many photographs of these trials show a small audience of brewery workers leaning on the fence to watch the fun and games.

Back at Wormwood Scrubs the little Killen-Strait was put through its paces at a special demonstration on 30 June. One of the biggest problems with the whole landship project was to explain it in simple terms to those in authority. The best way of doing this was to show the idea in action. Therefore, 20 Squadron laid on a show in front of a number of people, including Churchill and Lloyd George. Piles of railway sleepers and barricades of scrap metal were built up, which the Killen-Strait either climbed over or pushed down; the highlight of the demonstration was an assault upon a maze of barbed wire, the tractor equipped for the purpose with a set of naval net cutters. Dramatic as it was, the display did nothing to indicate the degree of progress made in landship design for, in reality there was virtually none to show for nearly six months of work, except in the negative sense of abandoned suggestions. However, fate held one more honour in store for the Killen-Strait, since it was later fitted with the body from a Delaunay-Belleville armoured car and probably became, albeit briefly, the first armoured tracklayer ever built.

To one member of the Landships Committee the poor results of all this varied experimental work was a considerable irritation. This was Albert Stern, a remarkable man from an influential banking family, who had joined the Royal Naval Air Service with the intention of raising a squadron of armoured cars. The chance to do this was passed before he was ready, so Sueter picked him to serve as secretary to the committee. Whatever the apparent responsibilities of this post may have been, Stern made sure that in reality he was soon virtually in charge. A strong character who was not afraid to make responsible decisions Stern had little time for military protocol. Consequently he trod hard on many toes but his urgent drive was desperately needed as the endless projects straggled on. As soon as he was sure of his authority, he acted fast and Crompton was one of the first casualties. The Colonel, in company with an associate, L. A. Legros, continued to produce drawings of articulated landships to lay before the committee but he was pursuing high engineering ideals which never showed any signs of reaching fruition. In order to help him, Stern had even transferred a young draughtsman, William Rigby, from Fosters to Kensington but the drawings he produced were described by Tritton as being little more than sketches, of no use in construction work. So Stern acted vigorously, dismissing Crompton and handing the entire project over to William Tritton at Lincoln. Rigby returned at once and Walter Wilson was sent to join Tritton with instructions to produce a working prototype as soon as possible, combining the Bullock tracks and Daimler power unit in a hull drawn by Rigby, which looked uncannily like half of one of the Crompton articulated landships.

There is no doubt that the old Colonel took it hard, yet he continued to produce designs and submit them, even after the first tanks had seen action. At the end of the war Legros attempted to restore his friend's reputation, even to the point of publishing a lengthy, technical article which somehow manages to trace the entire history of the invention of the tank with little more than passing references to Wilson and Tritton.

The set of specially extended Bullock tracks reached

7 *Although a blind alley, the Killen-Strait became, for a brief moment of glory, probably the first armoured tracklayer in the world. Commander Boothby, R.N.A.S., fitted it with the body of a Delaunay-Belleville armoured car.*

6 *At one stage Colonel Crompton favoured the idea of an articulated landship but the scheme foundered when trials of these two coupled Bullock tractors revealed severe handling problems.*

Liverpool docks early in August and were despatched at once to Lincoln. On seeing these tracks, both Wilson and Tritton doubted if they would prove suitable. They seemed too lightly constructed and these men were no doubt further influenced by a report from Field that mentioned the fact that the fitters in Chicago were in the habit of striking the track links with sledgehammers if they failed to match up exactly to the spacing of the sprocket teeth. Yet it was essential that the Landships Committee had something to show for the time and money it had consumed, so construction went ahead. It took one month of concentrated effort to complete the prototype tank and, on 10 September 1915, the Number I Lincoln Machine, as it was known, was ready for tests. It was an ungainly contraption to look at; the box-like hull, of riveted steel plates, rode above the frail track units while, at the rear, a pair of large wheels on a pivoting subframe, stuck out like a tail. These wheels were meant to act as a counterbalance during trench crossing and as a steering aid, acting like a ship's rudder, for making large radius turns. On top of the hull was a dummy turret intended to mount a two-pounder automatic cannon of the type known as a pom-pom, although for security reasons all this was draped with canvas covers. Inside the hull was the Daimler six-cylinder engine, two-speed gearbox and differential mechanism from a Foster-Daimler tractor. This drove a chain-and-sprocket arrangement that connected with the tracks. Steering was achieved, in addition to the tail method, by applying a brake to the half-shaft on one side or the other, so that two crewmen were required to drive it. One operated the engine controls while the other, sitting on the left side, worked the brake levers. The remaining members of the crew would work the main gun and the extra hull machine-guns that might be mounted. Trials at Cross-o-Cliffe Hill in Lincoln soon proved that the Bullock tracks were unsuitable. When the machine tried to cross a trench the tracks sagged away from the rollers and came off the frames, effectively disabling the vehicle altogether. Minor adjustments failed to improve it and the only answer was to design a new type as quickly as possible. Wilson and Tritton settled down in a room at the White Hart Hotel in the city, working late every night and filling the fireplace with the ashes of discarded ideas. Before long they had three schemes worthy of testing; multiple strands of cable, reinforced rubber conveyor belt and another system, the suggestion of William Tritton. This was the answer. There was nothing strikingly original about it, indeed simplicity and strength were the keynotes, but there were two unusual features. The

8 *The Number I Lincoln Machine, with Foster-built hull and Daimler engine, running on the special long set of Bullock tracks. Tarpaulins are draped over the dummy turret; the tail wheels are visible on the left.*

track rollers were not sprung at all but the spindles were anchored firmly to the frames. The tracks were formed with an internal lip that engaged runners in the frames and therefore could not drop away when unsupported. The tracks were formed from flat steel plates, riveted to cast inner links that were hinged together. Each plate was about 50cm (20in) wide and the joint between each pair was protected by an overlapping lip, which also served to provide some grip on soft ground.

On 30 November the new track frames were fitted to the Lincoln machine hull and the trials began again. Now known as 'Little Willie', the machine emerged from Foster's works without the temporary turret but with extra ballast added to increase the weight. The trials revealed that the designers had succeeded; the machine was slow and noisy, and the ride was anything but comfortable, but it worked. It was also completely obsolete.

Even before 'Little Willie' was finished a new idea had been conceived and the design work begun. Indeed, even before the new tracks had been designed it was realized that 'Little Willie' would not be able to conform to the latest War Office requirement, for, late in August, Stern had turned up at Lincoln with some firm demands tucked in his briefcase.

9 The new tracks, with their armoured frames, were soon fitted to the Lincoln Machine, which now became known as 'Little Willie'. It is seen at Wembley Park towards the end of the war, without the wheeled tail, which was found to be useless.

The War Office had finally realized that, like it or not, they were bound to inherit the Admiralty's brainchild before long so they decided that it might as well do exactly what was required of it. Based on the latest German practice in France, they stipulated that the new machine should be capable of lifting itself over a 1·37m (4ft 6in) parapet and cross a 2·5m (8ft) wide trench. These figures were almost double what the Landships Committee had been working on and they could only be met by drastically redesigning the whole machine. It is believed that Wilson actually came up with the answer, which was simply to enlarge the track frames until they were actually larger than the hull they supported. The frames were shaped like an irregular rhomboid, higher in the front than the rear, so that, on approaching an obstacle, the machine presented an elevated section of track to grip with. The hull between the tracks retained the basic box shape, with a raised cab at the front but, in order to avoid instability, the idea of a turret was rejected. Instead, the armament was housed in wedge-shaped casements, hung on both sides like panniers and referred to, in naval parlance, as sponsons. The guns, too, were of naval pattern. A number of potential weapons were considered and rejected either on the grounds of unsuitability or non-availability, so the choice finally settled on six-pounder naval guns, mounted one on each side, with a back-up of Hotchkiss machine-guns. Men from 20 Squadron built a wooden mock-up of the proposed design but, until a satisfactory track appeared, little could be done

12

to produce it. Once these were tested and found suitable the way was clear to build a machine whose shape was not dictated in any way by the strictures of a commercial track since everything would be built up from scratch.

One of the biggest problems now was the weight. The original model worked out at around 18 tons but Mother, as the new tank was called, would weigh about 28 tons. Fears were expressed that the two-speed transmission of 'Little Willie' would be overstrained so a system of supplementary gears was interposed between the differential and the final-drive sprockets. These secondary gears offered a further choice of two speeds and they also offered an alternative method of steering but they complicated the driving method alarmingly, since they could not be controlled directly by the driver. To deal with the steering, there were now three options open to the driver, depending on what he wanted to achieve. In the first place, a quick change of direction could be affected by having the commander, who sat on his left and also operated the track brakes, haul back on one lever, which stopped that track and swung the tank round. This, however, required considerable effort so it had to be used sparingly to avoid tiring him out. Secondly, the tail wheels could be used. By turning the wheel in the cab the driver caused the tail wheels to turn, like the front wheels of a car, and this forced the rear of the tank to swing outwards. This method, however, could only be used to make large radius turns and it would not work at all in certain conditions. Finally, he could use the secondary gears. Since these were located in the track frame, behind the sponsons, it was necessary to station two crewmen here to work the levers. On a signal from the driver, one man would engage neutral, leaving the track on the opposite side running and thus bringing the tank around. There were snags to this method: first, the driver's signals had to be clearly understood by the gearsmen, which was not easy in a dark and noisy tank, and, secondly, the extra mechanical parts were a potential source of extra trouble, for, if they became damaged in action, the tank was disabled completely.

In January 1916 the tank made its first move in Foster's yard. By the 20th it was declared ready and preliminary driving and firing trials were conducted. On the 29th it was taken down to Lord Salisbury's estate, Hatfield Park, just north of London, where a mock battlefield had been laid out, complete with trenches and shell holes of varying size. On 2 February, a demonstration was arranged, attended by Lloyd George, Lord Kitchener and many of those who had played a part in bringing the project to fruition. Mother behaved impeccably, crossing a 2·7m (9ft) trench and exceeding all expectations in the eyes of all but two onlookers. Lord Kitchener dismissed it as a 'pretty mechanical toy', with an aside to the effect that in his opinion the war would never be won by machines such as this. Colonel Crompton was more succinct; he called Mother 'The Slug'.

10 Early morning trials in a secluded park at Lincoln. A select group witness the first steps of Mother, the first machine to adopt the classic rhomboid shape which characterized most British tanks for the rest of the war.

CHAPTER II
1916, The First Tanks

The immediate response to the Hatfield Park demonstration was one of cautious optimism. Indeed, it would have been foolish to expect much else, with such a novel and unproven weapon. It is not surprising that Commodore Sueter ruffled a few military feathers that day by declaring his belief that 3000 tanks should be ordered at once. In the event, an order was placed for one hundred. It was clear, much as Tritton may have wished otherwise, that Fosters would be unable to build them all in a reasonable time so a bigger engineering firm, the Metropolitan Carriage, Wagon and Finance Company Ltd of Oldbury, Birmingham, was awarded the larger part of the contract. Walter Wilson was sent down there to act as official overseer. In due course the order was increased to 150, of which Fosters would build 25 and, at the same time, a variation was introduced. Considering the tanks in action, some people reasoned that while they were well enough equipped to deal with machine-gun posts and strongpoints, they lacked sufficient means to resist determined mass attack by infantry, or for that matter to clear infantry from trenches. For this reason it was decided to complete only half the order with tanks mounting six-pounders; the balance would be built with different sponsons to carry Vickers machine-guns only. To differentiate between the two, six-pounder tanks were styled as male machines and those armed with machine-guns as females. The new type of sponson was about the same size as the male pattern and so shaped that the machine-guns could sweep a large arc on each side of the tank. The main drawback was that this new shape did not allow for the full-size escape doors, which were fitted to the rear of the male sponson. The smaller escape doors designed instead proved almost impossible to use in a hurry. This problem would become crucial in the event of fire, and one of the worst features of these early tanks increased this risk considerably. The two 114-litre (25-gallon) petrol tanks were situated in the track frames at the front, on either side of the driver's cab. If a shell hit ruptured a fuel tank, the entire machine would be engulfed in seconds. Unless the men could escape quickly they were doomed. Fuel was fed to the engine by gravity, which is why the tanks were mounted so high, but if the machine got stuck, nose down in a trench or shell hole, this supply failed and the crew were forced virtually to hand-feed the engine to get it going again.

The Mark I heavy tanks that were the result of this first order were essentially the same as Mother. A few detail improvements were made but the most significant, from a service point of view, was that they were built of armoured plate, capable of resisting machine-gun fire, whereas Mother had been completed in unarmoured boiler plate. The armouring process was somewhat crude, since experience of making bullet-proof plate in such thin sheets (10mm thick at best on a Mark I) was very much an infant science. The plate was rolled, cut to size and drilled in its natural soft state and then hardened by a rapid heating and cooling process, before being attached to the frames with rivets.

Production was naturally slow at first but there were other matters to be solved in the meantime. Men had to be recruited to crew the tanks and the difficulty of doing this, when manpower was already such a problem, was compounded by the problem of being unable to tell the men exactly for what they were volunteering. In order to train in secret a large slice of land, hidden from public view, was required, and shortly found, on Lord Iveagh's estate at Elveden, near Thetford in Norfolk. Machine-gunners learnt their trade on the ranges at Bisley, near Camberley, and six-pounder gunners went to the Royal Navy's gunnery school at Whale Island in Portsmouth Harbour, H.M.S. *Excellent*.

New recruits arriving at Elveden found that the entire area had been sealed off and the civilian population evacuated. A team of Royal Engineers had prepared a replica of the German defence system, complete with shell holes, and a long railway siding had been laid so that the tanks could be delivered direct from the factories without having to travel by road. They also found that they had only one tank to train on. This was Mother, the first tank that many recruits ever saw. Others began to arrive in June 1916, until there were enough to provide six training tanks for each of the six companies destined to use them.

The establishment of the new unit was dictated by the number of tanks available, which, of course, had already been decided, along with the name by which the unit would be known. The first choice was the Tank Detachment, which must have sounded cryptic enough at the time but, just in case it revealed too much, it was soon changed to the Armoured Car Section, Motor Machine Gun Service. This sounded yet more revealing so, even before Elveden was open for business, it was changed, again, to the Heavy Section, Machine Gun Corps, a title it retained for the next six months. The six companies, A to F, which comprised the Heavy Section, were further subdivided into sections of four tanks each, with one extra tank per company to bring the total up to twenty-five. Colonel Swinton was appointed to command, as was only fitting, and he applied himself at once to devising training methods and a tactical basis for tank deployment. Given the novelty of the weapon, this was no mean task. All that could be done was to assess the job which had to be done and then apply military common sense within the bounds imposed by the limitations of the crude machines at his disposal. Accurate and careful gunnery, combined with techniques for communication and direction-finding were taught, while great stress was laid on the importance of surprise that could be exploited when the new arm was first used in battle. In so far as he could influence opinion at higher levels, Swinton did his best to impress the need for choosing ground suitable for the tank to work on and, in particular, to plead for restraint so that the first such attack should only take place when a sufficient number of tanks were ready, to be used *en masse*, rather than waste the potential element of surprise by premature exposure.

This would prove to be the stumbling block. The British Commander-in-Chief in France, Douglas Haig, began pestering Swinton for tanks as early as April. Plans were afoot for a major offensive to be launched on the Somme in July and Haig required some tanks to be ready in time to join in. As the time drew near, the pressure from France increased so that training had to be speeded up and eventually curtailed, but even then the deadline was passed. The Somme offensive which began on 1 July, set new records of slaughter in British military history. On the first day alone, 20,000 men were killed and 40,000 wounded; as the month wore on, losses were correspondingly high for very limited gains. Hitherto unequalled barrages of massed artillery failed to destroy the deep German defences and by August the crisis point had been reached. While the battle raged in France, another struggle was taking place at home; on one side the High Command stressed the need for even a limited number of tanks to boost the flagging offensive and tip the scales against German defence. On the other, those who had brought the tank so far, in the face of considerable opposition, pleaded for postponement, even until the following spring if necessary, in order to launch their surprise attack with the best possible chance of success. In this they were backed up by the French Army, who, with their own tanks now ready for production, did not want the chance of surprise pre-empted by the British and urged delay until a combined tank attack could be launched in 1917. The final arbiter was, however, Field Marshal Haig, and his order was that as many tanks as possible were to be ready, in France, in time for a renewed offensive to begin on 15 September 1916.

Frantic efforts were now being made to meet the new deadline. C Company arrived at the temporary training ground near Abbeville late in August, followed by D Company, which turned up just in time. A Company did not get to Abbeville before the eve of the attack and were therefore too late to see action. At the time, long distance movement of tanks was a nightmare. Since no suitable road transporters existed, all movement had to be done by rail and this entailed a great deal of work. In order to reduce the width of a tank sufficiently to stay within the loading gauge, the sponsons had to be unbolted and removed; they were transported separately on special trailers. These first deliveries to France went via Avonmouth Docks and Le Havre, loaded and unloaded from the ships by crane. They then went by rail over the French system until they reached the assembly area, where they were driven off and reunited with their sponsons. Here a new difficulty presented itself: without the sponsons, the hulls of some tanks had twisted so that when the sponson was offered up for refitting many of the bolt holes failed to line up and new ones had to be drilled. Many crews were exhausted even before they entered battle.

11 The dawn of a new era in warfare: British tanks prepare to go into action in September 1916. They are all Mark Is, fitted with the special grenade screens. A male tank is second from left with three female consorts.

As with all important débuts, there were problems. Natural teething troubles were aggravated by confusion and misunderstanding, brought about because those who thought they knew how tanks should be used outranked those who really did know, and consequently issued orders that demanded the impossible and wasted the potential. Of the sixty tanks available for this first battle, only forty-nine were in working order on the night of 14 September and, of these, only thirty-six made it as far as their starting points in time.

At 5.15 a.m. on 15 September 1916, the male tank D1, commanded by Captain H. W. Mortimore, moved out from its starting point near Ginchy and headed towards a German strong-point near Delville Wood. The two tanks that should have gone with it were not there. One had broken down and the other had got itself ditched behind the British line. Giving the tank a fifteen-minute start, two companies of the 6th Kings Own Yorkshire Light Infantry moved off in its wake, the men perhaps wondering at the dubious honour, arbitrarily conferred on them, of being the first troops ever to go into action with a tank. The thoughts of the German infantry, about to receive the even less inspiring distinction of being the first to face a tank in action are likewise unknown. If the enemy High Command had any inkling of what might be coming, they had not passed it down to the men in the trenches. All they could do was to make out an unearthly shape, lumbering over the broken ground apparently immune to their bullets. Every so often it paused, turned a little as if sniffing the air, and came on again. The guns waved about as the gunner's sought their targets, steadied, fired and resumed the waving. In the centre of the cab a Hotchkiss machine-gun fired short bursts whenever the unseen commander could afford to take his hands off the steering brakes. Some men fought and fell, others ran. D1 arrived at the enemy line, deserted now but for the dead, and waited for the infantry to come up. At this point its career came to an abrupt end when a shell, either from an enemy gun or the British barrage, struck the steering gear and put it out of action.

Just after 6 a.m. the remaining tanks got under way. The barrage, which had already churned up the ground, now opened up to leave lanes along which the tanks were to advance, although cases are on record of British shells knocking out a few tanks, while others broke down or became ditched and were therefore lost, at least for the duration. Survivors' recollections tend to dwell more upon the difficulties of keeping their tanks rolling than on actual fighting, which was probably just as well, for many of them were in action for the first time. Concentrating on the job in hand probably prevented the men from being overwhelmed by the variety of unpleasant sensations that threatened them, although some of these would have become familiar through training. Inside every tank eight men were cooped up; at least four of them had seats but the six-pounder crews were obliged to crouch since there was insufficient headroom for the average man to stand upright. Every orifice was closed to prevent bullets from getting in so the available light was minimal. The heat from the engine was intense and many of the pipes nearby were too hot to touch. The air was full of carbon monoxide fumes and burnt cordite and the noise was deafening. The roar of the engine, the screech of the tracks and the crash of the guns made speech impossible so, when the driver wanted a secondary gear to be changed, he banged loudly on the engine casing to attract attention and indicated with his fingers which gear to engage. All this time the tank was rolling and writhing as it crossed the uneven ground and then it would pitch into a shell hole throwing everyone off balance. On top of all this, the tank was soon a target for every machine-gun and rifle that could be brought to bear. Bullets splattered like rain on the hull and, when they found a gap, droplets of molten lead squirted through to splash the skin or damage the eyes. Special face masks, half leather, half chain-mail, had been issued, along with hardened leather skull caps, but they were not popular and the men tended to leave them off. The gunner peered through his telescope as it bounced around, looking for a target. If the machine was moving, the best he could hope for was a chance shot which often went wide of the mark. The commander and driver watched the outside world through glass vision blocks which were easily shattered by bullets, or through slim periscopes that stuck out through the roof of the cab. If the engine stalled, the men had to spring to the starting handle and crank it furiously until it fired. The gravity petrol feed often failed to function when the tank was stuck nose down in a hole. Great care was then required to prime the engine by hand before it could be restarted and all movement was tricky because the floor was soon awash with spent machine-gun cartridge cases that slithered to and fro.

Any comfort the men took from their armoured protection, when compared with the hapless infantry, was short-lived if a shell struck and set them alight. In theory escape was possible via a manhole in the roof or through the sponson doors but, on the female tanks, these doors were so small that rapid evacuation was impossible. There are cases recorded of small men wriggling through the lookout ports in the front of the cab, although in some instances losing their clothes in the process, for the threat of fire is a great stimulant. Once outside, of course, they were no better off than the infantry. Indeed, their case was worse if they were seen by enraged and frightened enemy gunners so the nearest shell hole was sought out as a refuge.

The day was one of local surprise rather than overwhelming victory; some tanks did extremely well but the one that caught the public imagination was Lieutenant Hastie's D17, nicknamed 'Dinnaken', which penetrated the enemy-held village of Flers and put the defenders to flight. But it was the failures that were remembered by the rest of the Army. Many thus dismissed the tanks as an overrated gimmick, a posture that was also adopted by the German High Command for rather different reasons. In order to play down the effect of surprise and the resulting panic which soon spread well behind the front, they spoke in deprecating tones which soon gained wide currency while, in secret, they began to plan a tank force of their own.

Over the next few days the surviving tanks were used again and again in an effort to consolidate the gains and capture more ground. However, the offensive was running out of steam; by the end of the month, the prolonged and costly Battle of the Somme was effectively over.

Anyone who had watched those first tanks climbing aboard the trains at Foster's factory, and had then seen them again in France a few months later, would have been struck at once by a couple of changes. To begin with, the plain grey sides of the hulls had been embellished with a varied pattern of camouflage colours, which made them look like discarded artists' palettes. This was the result of work by the Royal Academician Solomon J. Solomon, now a Lieutenant-Colonel of the Royal Engineers, who had accepted the surprising commission of devising a disruptive camouflage scheme, intended to break up the distinctive outline. The other addition was the bomb roof, a gabled wooden framework covered in wire netting, which was mounted above the tank in order to deflect hand grenades and prevent them from exploding on top of the hull. In the end it was decided that this addition was more trouble than it was worth and it did not reappear in 1917.

If the performance of these first tanks had disappointed many who had expected much more from them, it seems that Haig, at least, was not so dismayed. On 19 September he requested, through the War Office, that a further 1000 tanks be ordered and, while this was being arranged, an interim order for 100 training tanks was placed, both to keep the factories going and to provide a nucleus of suitable training machines for the extra crews that would be needed to man them.

Meanwhile the two original companies in France, supplemented by A Company, endeavoured to keep the tanks in action. Throughout October a series of small and relatively ineffective actions were fought, culminating, in November, in a larger operation at Beaumont-Hamel, where they supported the 63rd (Royal Naval) Division under Colonel C. B. Freyberg. The point chosen for the attack was on the very left flank of the old Somme battlefield where the July offensive had met its bloodiest reverse. Some forty tanks made a surprise dawn attack in thick mist. Freyberg was awarded a Victoria Cross for his efforts in the battle, which only ended when the Germans were driven out of Beaumont, leaving their flanks dangerously exposed.

With winter coming on, the chance for further action was passed until next spring and a period of consolidation ensued. In France a permanent headquarters was established for the new force at the village of Bermicourt, around which grew up, over the next few months, a vast complex of repair shops, tank parks and training schools.

12 The Mark I male tank D7 (No. 742) of Lieutenant Enoch at rest after the Flers action. Notice the camouflage scheme, the circular roof hatch and the two periscopes above the cab. Three crew members can be seen wearing the hardened leather crash helmets.

Central Workshops, and anti-gas and compass schools were laid out at Erin. Driver training was done at Wailly, wireless and signals at Fleury and the maintenance school was in Bermicourt itself. Gunnery training was conducted on the coast at Merlimont, while the tanks were stored both in sheds and in the open at Rollencourt. Command of the tanks in France was placed in the hands of Lieutenant-Colonel Hugh Elles, a brilliant young officer who had been associated with the formation of the new arm while serving as Haig's link man, keeping an eye on developments in Britain. Elles' style of personal leadership did much to foster a spirit of personal unity and purpose among the diverse elements that were attracted to the tanks and he was supported by an enthusiastic staff. Recruitment had begun again once the need for expansion had been agreed and soon adventurous spirits from all the armed forces were heading for Bermicourt to join up. In November the unit title was changed once again to the Heavy Branch, Machine Gun Corps, while officially the cap badge remained the crossed Vickers guns appropriate to that unit. However, many volunteers continued, for the time at least, to sport the uniform and badge of their original regiment so a cloth arm badge, in the shape of a tank, was adopted for those members of the Corps qualified to take their place in a tank crew. At the same time the original company system was changed to one of battalions, each with three companies which comprised, in due course, four sections with four tanks apiece. These battalions inherited the identifying letters originally instituted for the companies.

Back in Britain it was clear that an expanded Corps would need more room than was available in Norfolk. A new location was sought, and duly found, on a vast area of uncultivated heathland near Wool in Dorset. Bovington Camp had, until then, served as a temporary training ground for local regiments but it had a small nucleus of permanent accommodation and there was plenty of room for tents. Tank training was conducted on the heath, where special courses were laid out, while the nearby coastal settlement at Lulworth became the home of the Gunnery School. Later in the war the towns of Wareham and Swanage had detached camps of their own.

The small bridging order for 100 tanks, placed in September, was divided equally into two types, Marks II and III. Although they were essentially the same as the original Mark I, each incorporated a number of minor improvements indicated as necessary in the first actions.

13 Tank Corps Central Workshops in France. In the foreground there is a vast dump of Tadpole Tail assemblies destined never to be used. Among the tanks in the background can be seen three of the little French Renaults that were used by the Corps and some infantry units as liaison machines.

Each mark was again subdivided into equal numbers of male and female types but, since they were only intended for training, no attempt was made to armour the hull plates. The Mark IIs had slightly narrower cabs than the Mark Is, since there were plans under consideration to fit the tanks with wider tracks. The flat manhole hatch in the hull roof was replaced by a wedge-shaped structure, incorporating a hatch, which provided better protected vision for the crew. In order to investigate the possibility of improving armour protection, the plates of the Mark II were made with extra holes which, it was hoped, would be used to rivet on an extra layer of plate, but this practice was rejected for the Mark III, in favour of using thicker (12mm) plate on certain vulnerable areas. To the casual observer, however, the most obvious change in tank design was the absence of the tail wheels. They had proved to be more of a liability than a help on active service and the tanks behaved just as well without them, so they soon disappeared from the Mark Is and were not adopted for subsequent models. Most of these features, along with a series of detailed improvements, were incorporated in the Mark IV when it entered production, while Marks II and III began to arrive at Bovington towards the end of 1916.

Just before the year ended there were two significant changes concerning personnel. For reasons that were never entirely specified, Swinton was removed from the overall command of the Corps and returned to his job at the War Office. Brigadier-General F. Gore Anley took his place but throughout the war the appointment was overshadowed by the fighting branch in France. There, at Bermicourt, the staff was increased with the arrival of Major J. F. C. Fuller, who took up the post of General Staff Officer. A brilliant and unconventional officer, Fuller soon became a powerhouse of tactical and strategic ideas which had far-reaching effects on the future conduct of armoured warfare.

14 A pair of female Mark IIIs at Bovington during a training run. The nearest tank carries the old type Vickers gun sponson, while the one in the background has the new Lewis pattern with large escape doors below.

15 A Mark III male tank in Britain demonstrates unditching techniques. This close-up view shows the early type of exhaust baffles and the wedge-shaped hatch that replaced the round manhole of the Mark I.

16 Mass production of tanks began with the Mark IV in 1917. This male tank shows how to cross a light railway without wrecking it. Notice the smaller sponson, shorter gun and the unditching beam at the rear.

17 The Mark IV female tank 2559 in the ruined village of Peronne. It provides a clear view of the unditching beam and the extension track plates, or grousers, stowed in the tray on the roof.

CHAPTER III
1917, Expansion and Fulfilment

Field Marshal Haig's order for 1000 more tanks was both timely and premature: timely in that it expressed the Commander-in-Chief's faith in the new arm, in the face of considerable scepticism, but premature, since it was placed before sufficient improvements were agreed upon the original design. Thus the Mark IV tank was only altered in relatively minor details over the Mark I. Six hundred of the new type were to enter production as soon as all the Mark II and III models were delivered, on a ratio of two female to one male, while the balance of 400 was held back with a view to incorporating such improvements as might be decided later. The majority were again to be built in Birmingham while Fosters made their share and two more factories, the Coventry Ordnance Works in Glasgow and Armstrong-Whitworths at Newcastle, joined the production team later.

Among the immediate improvements agreed for the Mark IV was a relocation of the fuel tanks in a safer spot outside the hull at the rear, where they were protected by the track frames. Now that the wheeled tail was no longer in use there was plenty of room in this area, but it also meant that a more efficient system of petrol delivery, known as the Autovac, had to be used to replace the gravity feed. Another feature ready for improvement was the engine exhaust. In fact, the Mark I type can be said to have had no exhaust system whatever, just a series of baffle plates on the hull top through which smoke, sparks and, above all, noise escaped in profusion, making the tank a focal point for enemy attention. The Mark IV was, therefore, fitted with a silencer, which was connected to an exhaust pipe that carried the tell-tale fumes away and dispersed them at the rear.

The long six-pounder guns were replaced, in the new mark, by shorter ones, less prone to damage through striking obstacles or getting clogged up with mud. Furthermore, the tiresome business of unbolting and removing sponsons for rail travel was disposed of by making the sponson slightly smaller so that it could be pushed inboard to reduce the overall width. The shape of the male sponson was also changed to present a narrower frontage, less likely to bury itself in the mud on soft ground. The change in the female sponson was even more dramatic. Initially, this change was because of a decision to replace the heavy Vickers machine-guns with a lighter type. The advantage of standardizing secondary armament was obvious, simply on the grounds of economic ammunition stowage. The Hotchkiss was perfectly adequate for tank use but the War Office chose to listen to the advice of a machine-gun expert, who had no experience of tanks, when he recommended the adoption of the Lewis gun instead. Admirable as this American weapon was in the field, it did not behave well in tanks; the engine fan tended to draw fumes from the gun straight into the gunner's face, making accurate shooting impossible, while the barrel jacket was easily damaged by small-arms fire. It was replaced, in time, by another version of the Hotchkiss but, until then, the crews had to suffer. With the adoption of a lighter machine-gun, of whatever type, it now became possible to design a lighter female sponson in which to mount it. It was a slim structure, shaped like a small bow window, which only occupied the upper half of the hull opening, so a large pair of escape doors were fitted below. These sponsons could be folded inboard for rail travel.

Another important innovation that appeared with the Mark IV was the unditching beam. This handy device replaced a variety of improvised systems employed by tank crews for getting their machines on the move once they had become bogged in a shell hole or stuck in glutinous mud. The unditching beam, which was supported on rails which ran along the top of the hull, took the form of a large oak beam, clad in metal, which could be chained to the tracks and hauled round with them as they slithered ineffectually on soft ground. Once the beam wedged itself beneath the tank, the tracks had something to bite on and the machine was able to lever itself out of trouble, moving forwards until the beam passed underneath and returned to its place on the rails. The only disadvantage was that, in order to attach or disconnect the chains, an unfortunate volunteer had to expose himself to the rain of machine-gun fire and fumble with the muddy shackles.

The transition from experimental to full-scale production meant that the Landships Committee had fulfilled its purpose and, in the early part of 1916, it had become the Tank Supply Department of the Ministry of Munitions. In March both Stern and Wilson relinquished their naval appointments and became majors in the Army, while a number of other RNAS personnel changed service at the same time. By the summer Stern was finding it increasingly irksome to work with a committee breathing down his neck and proposed certain changes which, in effect, put him in full control of tank production in Britain. It was a good time to have a firm hand on the tiller but Stern's autocratic ways often upset important people and on a few occasions he made arbitrary decisions that were of questionable value in the long run. One such was to authorize the construction of even more Mark IV tanks, bringing the total to 1400, of which in due course, more than 1200 were completed. This meant that throughout the war the Mark IV was far and away the most common type in British service and it tended to delay development of improved models that were waiting in the wings until production lines were ready for them. This error of judgement was used later, by his enemies, to engineer his removal from office. It was also unfortunate that he allowed himself to decide on engineering matters about which he had very little knowledge and this, too, on one occasion, had very serious consequences. Shortly after the first tank actions on the Somme, Stern and Wilson went over to France with other members of the committee and representatives of 20 Squadron. They saw the tanks at the front and then went on to visit the French tank factories and examine their work. As a result of this visit the engineer in the party, Walter Wilson, realized that a simpler form of control for the tanks was an urgent requirement. Nobody disagreed with him, least of all the tank crews, for the effort required to work the steering levers was considerable and it handicapped the commander in performing his other duties. Likewise steering on the gears was a tiresome business complicated by communication difficulties and mechanical problems. Wilson's solution, worked out more or less on the spot, was to substitute an epicyclic drive, which permitted one-man control and worked by applying brakes to a rotary gear system, which altered the speed of one track or the other. Unable to grasp such technical theory, Stern was more impressed by what he could actually see, the petrol-electric drive train of the St Chamond tank, so he overruled Wilson, much to the latter's annoyance. Stern was at least open-minded enough to consider alternatives and, since the existence of tanks was no longer a secret, he felt inclined to invite suggestions from other inventors who might have better ideas. He organized a comparative trial of all rival systems for March 1917, and released five of the new Mark II models from the production lines to serve as test beds. There were in fact six contenders because the prototype tank, Mother, was also included, being refitted by Daimlers with their own version of the petrol-electric drive. One Mark II was sent to France for the installation of the St Chamond system while the four others were fitted with transmissions known as the Williams-Janney Hydraulic, Westinghouse Petrol-Electric, Wilkins Multiple Clutch and, of course, Wilson's Epicyclic.

On 3 March 1917, the competing designs attended at the Oldbury testing ground in Birmingham to be judged; all that is, except the St Chamond, which was still not ready. A new Mark IV, straight from the factory, was included for comparative purposes and Mother attended, despite the fact that the Daimler equipment had proved unsuitable on earlier trials. Each tank was marked with a different colour for the benefit of the on-lookers and one wonders what Stern must have thought, after watching the white tank, which was clearly the best, when he glanced down at his programme to find that it was Wilson's Epicyclic. Had he

18 This Mark II tank was modified to take a Westinghouse-designed petrol electric transmission for the Oldbury Trials in March 1917. Notice that the engine has been moved rearwards.

listened to his expert engineer in the first place it is altogether possible that the new transmission could have been available for the Mark IV. Two other designs were on show at Oldbury, a faster light tank, built at Fosters and called, after its designer, the Tritton Chaser, and a prototype for a self-propelled artillery transporter based loosely on the Mark I tank.

19 The engine of this Mark II was moved forwards to leave more room for the hydraulic Williams-Janney transmission, which was also tested at Oldbury. It had three extra radiators at the back to improve cooling. Seen later in the war at Wembley Park, it is parked beside the amphibious Mark IX Duck.

Another design from this period, which had nothing to do with Oldbury, never got much beyond the drawing-board stage. This was the 'Flying Elephant'. The nickname was applied to a heavily armoured machine, conceived by William Tritton in response to a request for an assault tank that would be proof against field artillery. In overall size it was little different from a Mark I, but the body was formed as a dome-shaped carapace in 50mm thick plate, mounting a six-pounder gun at the front and three machine-guns on either side. Power was to be provided by a pair of Daimler engines, since the estimated weight was in the region of 100 tons, and, in order to spread the weight, the main driving

20 The Oldbury Trials, held in March 1917 saw the début of the Tritton Chaser, a faster, lighter medium tank for cavalry work.

21 A Mark I male tank in Gaza bearing the name H.M.L.S. Ole Luke Oi, the pen-name of Ernest Swinton, first commander of the Tank Corps.

tracks were supplemented by an inner pair, which came into action on soft ground. Work began on the engines, but the requirement was later dropped and the tank was never completed.

While all this was going on in Britain, preparations were being made in France for a new offensive. No actions were planned before the spring, when, it was hoped, the weather would have improved, the ground would be dry and a mass of new tanks would have been delivered. In the meantime eight old training tanks, Mark Is from Britain, were detached from E Battalion and sent out to Egypt with their crews, where they arrived in January 1917. It was thought at first that they would not operate effectively on sand, but they were quick to disprove this and were duly sent to Palestine to join the attack on Turkish positions at Gaza, but the battle was abandoned before they were ready. They took part in a second attack which was mounted in April with some success, although three of them were destroyed, while the remainder were withdrawn to await developments.

Plans for the spring offensive in France were disrupted by the Germans who, late in February, began to pull back to newly prepared positions in what the Allies called the Hindenburg Line on the Somme front. Revised plans, therefore, called for an assault in the Arras area, further north. Delays in delivery of the new Mark IV meant that Central Workshops had to work round the clock, getting as many Mark Is as possible fit for action. As an emergency measure, Bovington released twenty-six Mark II training tanks, which brought the effective strength of C and D Battalions up to sixty machines, but these unarmoured reinforcements were extremely vulnerable, the more so since the Germans had by now developed an effective anti-tank bullet for small arms. There was still snow on the ground when the attack began on 9 April, after a three-week artillery barrage that was supposed to 'soften-up' the defence. All it managed to do was to soften-up the ground and advertise, for the Germans' benefit, exactly where the blow would fall. On the eve of battle six tanks were temporarily lost to C Battalion when they became immobilized in a swamp near Achicourt while taking a short cut to the front. The remaining tanks put up a fine show, assisted by a well co-ordinated barrage and effective infantry support. The enemy front line was in British hands within the hour but this promise of quick success was not fulfilled on succeeding days. The German positions had been prepared in great depth, creating a cushion effect which did not rely on a single line, so the further the tanks advanced the more resistance they met. In addition, adequate artillery support was not forthcoming, since it proved impossible to bring the guns up over the well-churned ground and the lighter pieces were unable to range on German rear positions. Gradually the attack petered out as fewer and fewer tanks remained capable of fighting on, while the cavalry, who had been brought forward to exploit the breakthrough, halted when they came up against a wall of fire. The final nail came with a proposed attack on Bullecourt. Here the tanks failed to reach their starting points on the 10th, which caused unnecessary casualties among the Australian infantry who were to work with them. On the following day, many more Australian lives were lost when the troops followed the tanks over snow-covered ground in the face of hostile fire. Tanks and men were silhouetted against the snow; eight out of eleven tanks were knocked out, while the infantry were cut down in droves. An attempt to renew the offensive later in the month saw the surviving tanks in action again, but the limited gains were obtained at great cost. Thus it seemed, to those in command, that the new engine of war had failed to live up to its promise. While the factories in Britain strove to complete the thousand and more new tanks, the tide of professional opinion swung against them. Things would not improve for six months, since the arena chosen by Haig for his summer

22 The Mark II male tank Lusitania during the battle of Arras. This photograph is of particular interest since it was autographed by many of the famous names associated with the creation of the tank, including D'Eyncourt, Wilson, Tritton and Stern.

23 A female Mark II ditched in the uncongenial surroundings of a peacetime graveyard. The Lewis guns are gone, since the crew were expected to abandon a ditched tank and fight alongside the infantry in these circumstances.

offensive, the water-logged Flanders plain, was quite unsuitable for the tanks. That Haig saw this northern flank, around Ypres, as the decisive theatre of operations, is clear from his comments at the start of the year, and he would attack there come what may. If his chosen battleground was not suitable for tanks, then what use were tanks? Haig's plans were therefore formulated as if on the premise that tanks did not exist.

The Mark IVs began to arrive in France in May. They arrived without the unditching beams and rails, which had to be fabricated at Central Workshops, putting an extra strain on that already stretched organization. They were also painted all over in a medium brown colour, Solomon's exotic camouflage having proved ineffective, especially since it was soon covered in mud anyway. Meanwhile most of the surviving male tanks of the Mark I type were converted to Supply Tenders. The conversion involved removal of the guns and plating over of the aperture. The sponson was then available for loading with stores, fuel and, ammunition. Once the battle zone had been crossed by tanks it was not only the artillery that found it impassable. No lorry or horse-drawn wagon could get across either, so reserves of munitions and such like had to be carried by huge parties of men, who wound along the slippery board-walks and occasionally slipped into a water-filled shell hole to disappear forever. One supply tank could carry enough to replenish five fighting tanks.

In June there was another change of title when the Heavy Branch was renamed the Tank Corps. A new badge, a male tank enclosed by a wreath, replaced the crossed machine-guns and, since January, men of each battalion wore a distinguishing coloured flash on the shoulder. At the same time pairs of battalions had been brigaded and, following Arras, F and G Battalions came to France to be paired with the depleted survivors of those battles. Each battalion now received six Mark I supply tanks in addition to its normal establishment. Including the two in Britain, there were now nine battalions in all, and four more were added by August. In addition to a collective personality, the Tank Corps was beginning to identify its individual characters, one of whom was the Intelligence Officer, Captain F. E. Hotblack. Many contend that some of the deeds he performed under fire were worthy of the Victoria Cross, but this was not awarded and much of his diligent work went almost unnoticed. However, standards he set for reconnaissance work established a tradition that was readily honoured by his contemporaries in both word and deed. The need for an accurate survey of the battle ground was of vast importance to the tanks. Even before they reached the British lines to begin the attack it was vital that their routes be chosen with the greatest of care, and this had to be continued as far into the actual battlegound as possible. Much of the preparation for an attack had to be done in the dark, so chosen routes were marked out with luminous tape, while tanks were often guided forward by men on foot who wore special jackets with red and green lights attached to the back. Officers found it helpful to carry with them a long stick in order to test the firmness of the ground. This established a tradition, still maintained, for Royal Tank Regiment officers to carry a representative 'Ash Plant' in place of the normal swagger cane. These small symbols and peculiarities were gradually giving the Corps an identity, but what it needed most was a reputation. Now, with a nucleus of experienced veterans, and a serviceable if uninspired tank, it awaited the chance.

On 7 June the attack on Messines Ridge was launched as a preliminary to the Third Battle of Ypres. The centrepiece of this battle was a huge explosion of nineteen underground mines, which so dismayed the Germans that the infantry gained most of their objectives with little help from the tanks. In any case, these had been accorded a very small part in the overall scheme. The début of the Mark IV was, therefore, a very muted affair, although the crews were pleased to find the extra frontal armour proof against the new German armour-piercing bullet. Examination of tanks destroyed around Arras had convinced the Germans that they now had a suitable antidote to the tank, for the Mark IIs, of course, had been penetrated repeatedly. This confidence lasted for quite a long time and proved a small boon to the Tank Corps in that difficult summer. A fifteen-day artillery bombardment preceded the Ypres battle, which was launched on 31 July. Heavy rain began to fall on the same day and, before long, the low-lying Yser valley was virtually awash. Neither infantry nor tanks could make much progress against these elements, let alone against the Germans who occupied the higher ground to the east. After three months of fighting, at a cost of some quarter of a million men, four miles of all but impassable ground had been wrested from the enemy. It ended early in November, in the ruins of a village, the very name of which sounds like a protesting cry; the village was called Passchendaele.

Even in this tale of unremitting tragedy, which brought the Tanks Corps to a new low in professional esteem, there were some bright spots. At St Julien in the middle of August, a special company from G Battalion executed a brilliant little operation on firm ground, without any preliminary bombardment. Tanks subdued two major German fieldworks for minimal casualties to themselves and the infantry they supported. In September Captain Clement Robertson won the first Victoria Cross awarded to the corps during the war, for some cool-headed reconnaissance work that cost him his life.

Another pointer to the future was encapsulated in an ingenious plan which was unfolding at Tank Corps Headquarters. This plan, had it been mounted, could have added a new dimension to the prospects of tank warfare. The northern sector of the line, on which the Ypres battlefield lay, included a feature rare in Western Front topography, an open flank. This, of course, was the Belgian coastline, which, to a maritime nation, should have been a natural extension of their fighting territory. Plans had been mooted for its exploitation before but, until the advent of the tank, this had been limited to sporadic naval bombardment. Now, with the proximity of the new battlefront it began to assume a new importance. A scheme was hatched whereby a small force of all arms, including nine tanks, would be put ashore behind the German lines in order to link up with the advance of the main British Army from Ypres to take Ostend. The landing force would be divided into three sections of roughly equal composition, and each section would be landed from an enormous pontoon, which would be pushed ashore by a pair of monitors—shallow draught warships, mounting large calibre guns—with the tanks in the van to silence any opposition. The main physical obstacle was the sloping sea-wall, which was too steep and too slippery to be climbed without assistance. In order to achieve this a special training area was set up at Merlimont, complete with a replica section of wall, and some special equipment was developed.

The initial difficulty of actually climbing the wall was solved by adding special claws to the tank tracks, which dug through the slippery seaweed and into the fabric of the wall. In order to heave themselves over the lip at the top, each tank pushed before it a small portable ramp, which was forced against the lip and served as a means of climbing over it. The female tank in each group of three was further equipped with a special winch mounted outside the hull on the right. By stationing itself on top of the wall, this tank could haul up the lorries, guns and stores that the force would require, while her male consorts were subduing the immediate opposition. All this equipment was prepared, including the pontoons, and the participants trained to a fine pitch, but the 'Hush Operation', as it was called, was never mounted. The failure of the Ypres offensive ruined any chance there might have been for the two forces to join up. Even so, it remains a most interesting addition to the annals of amphibious warfare and a remarkable tribute to the potential of the tank within a year of its first use in action.

In Britain expansion of the Corps was reflected in improvements to the process of inspection and delivery. A testing station, controlled by the men of 20 Squadron RNAS, had been established close to each production centre, the main one being at Oldbury. Here each tank was put through its paces and entrained for the front. Delivery was via Southampton and Le Havre, where the naval delivery party handed over their charges to the Army. There were mechanical improvements, too; a young naval officer, Lieutenant W. O. Bentley, devised a means of improving the performance of the Daimler engine by increasing the compression to the point where it delivered 125hp. Notwithstanding Bentley's later success as a racing-car designer, his improved engines turned out to be temperamental in action, so that most of the 100 or more tanks fitted with them were relegated to supply carrying duties.

The gun-carrier machine that attended the Oldbury trials in March had also been developed. Fifty were built by Kitson and Co of Leeds and they started arriving in France in June. The track frames were low, surmounted at the rear by a box-shaped hull that contained the engine and drive train along with members of the crew. The driver and brakesman occupied small one-man cabs nearer the front. The forward section was an open well, containing a sliding cradle to carry the gun, which was loaded by means of power-operated winches connected to the engine. Two types of gun could be handled, the six-inch howitzer, or the sixty-pounder field gun but, on account of the recoil, only the

25 This Mark IV supply tank also demonstrates the field-recovery techniques adopted during the war. It is shown righting a Mark V that has suffered an internal explosion.

24 A Mark IV male tank with a portable ramp on the training wall at Merlimont.

26 The gun carriers rarely saw service in their intended role but Darlington is seen here, mounting a 6-inch howitzer and fully kitted out for war. Notice the gun wheels slung on the side of the hull.

former could be fired from this mounting. In either case, the gun wheels were first removed and hung on the sides of the hull when the piece was winched in place, while ammunition could be stored both within and on top of the rear hull section. Since the design dated from 1916, the carriers first appeared with tail wheels, but these were soon discarded, and in fact the carriers were rarely used in their intended role. The idea was sound enough: guns could now be brought forward across the captured ground directly behind the tanks and then used to lay down a barrage in support of the next stage of the advance. But the gunners seemed loath to trust their precious weapons to the tank men, and the idea never caught on. Instead, the machines were relegated to supply work, a role in which they soon outshone the converted tanks, on account of their greater capacity. Two of them were completed as salvage machines, mounting hand-operated cranes in place of the gun, while at a later stage, the Royal Engineers used the frames of a carrier as the basis for a mobile steam grab-crane for earth-moving.

Many conventional tanks were modified for salvage work, with a simple jib and purchase mounted on the front of the track frames. They were used mainly at base workshops to assist in the lifting of heavy components and, to a limited extent, for field recovery. When the Germans constructed the Hindenburg Line, they paid particular attention to defence against tanks. In addition to barrage-proof dug-outs in the front line, a system of reserve trenches had been prepared, each with its own maze of barbed wire and many of these trenches had been widened sufficiently to prevent a tank from getting across. A simple yet effective method of overcoming this was the fascine, a large round bundle of brushwood, tightly bound with chains, which was carried above the cab of the tank and released into the trench to form a sort of stepping stone that succeeding tanks could use. Although this piece of equipment was used on numerous occasions, it had one disadvantage in that, once it had been dropped, it could not be recovered and used again. The obvious alternative was to lengthen the tank, and

Fosters found a means of doing this with what they called the 'Tadpole Tail'. It consisted of a prefabricated extension of the track frames at the rear, which could be bolted on to any tank, along with the extra track links that went with it. Trench-crossing ability was improved, trials indicated that a 3·6m (12ft) trench could be bridged, but also showed that the structure was altogether too flexible, and liable to twist out of shape in service, so it was never used in action. However, a large number of tails were made and shipped to France.

The small tank detachment in Palestine was brought up to strength with the arrival of three Mark IV machines, and the unit took part in General Allenby's Third Battle of Gaza. This succeeded in containing Turkish attention while the cavalry undertook a vast outflanking movement. From then on, the war in this region became highly mobile and there was nothing more for the tanks to do. They were duly returned to Egypt, while the unit was disbanded and the men returned to France.

While the Ypres battle had pursued its tragic course, the

28 The Royal Engineers converted one gun carrier into a mechanical digger mounting a steam powered Priestman grab. The crane's steam unit also provided motive power for the chassis and the gears were operated by men walking alongside.

29 Female Mark IV tank No. 2739 is fitted with the Portable Tank Crane attachment on its nose. It is unloading a tank engine from a small railway wagon at Central Workshops.

27 One of two gun carriers converted into salvage machines. The hand-operated crane is on a platform over the gun well, with the raised driving cab beyond it. Sheerlegs, used to increase the lifting capacity, are stowed on the sides; the external winding drum is also visible.

30 Trench crossing was never easy. This Mark IV female demonstrates how not to do it.

31 The Germans countered the tanks with wider trenches. One solution to this was the Tadpole Tail, seen here applied to a Mark IV. The painted line on the hull shows the limit of the original tank, but the extension proved too flexible for operational use and never saw action.

32 Mark IV tanks also appeared in Gaza, where this one is about to board a train behind a sponson-less Mark I.

senior staff of the Tank Corps had been planning. To those who could see the potential of the tank, the twelve months of wasted employment appeared to verge upon the criminal. First among these visionaries was J. F. C. Fuller. Once he became convinced of the value of armoured warfare, he started to devise schemes for its proper use, his ideas being re-enforced by what he saw in Flanders. His dramatic scheme, for an attack towards St Quentin in September, was designed around the tank as the key piece on the field. This plan which it was hoped would restore British confidence and French esteem, was somewhat modified by his superiors, until it became a glorified raid against Cambrai, a German-held town along the road from Arras, in November. The tank remained the principal element in the attack and, as far as possible, the activities of all other arms would be subordinated to it. It would rely on surprise, for there would be no preparatory barrage, and overwhelming strength. All nine battalions of the Tank Corps then in France were to take part, a combined force of over 300 tanks, supported by five infantry divisions and five cavalry divisions.

The logistical problems alone were immense. To assemble the tanks in the area, the Railway Operating Department had to arrange for thirty-six trains, each carrying twelve tanks, and lay many miles of sidings at a temporary railhead called Spree Farm. Loading and unloading the tanks was a nightmare in itself. A ramp was erected at the end of a siding and a line of flat wagons drawn up against it. One by one the tanks climbed aboard from the end and made their way, unsteadily, from wagon to wagon. With the tracks overhanging the sides of the wagons, there was no room for error so the drivers relied entirely on men guiding them from ahead. At the destination the whole process was repeated as the tanks drove off and then the crew set to work sliding out the sponsons and setting up the armament. All this was carried out in the utmost secrecy, usually in the dark; this time there had to be total surprise.

Before dawn on 20 November the tanks were drawn up on the downs overlooking Cambrai. Ahead of them lay firm, unspoiled country leading to the Hindenburg Line. Close to the centre of the six-mile line of tanks stood a male Mark IV of H Battalion, the inappropriately named Hilda. Towards this tank, through the pre-dawn mist, strode the tall figure of Brigadier-General Hugh Elles. He climbed aboard Hilda and proceeded to unroll a brown, red and green flag which he displayed from the tank. These colours, chosen almost at random, were taken by Fuller to signify mud, blood and the green fields beyond, towards which the tanks were aiming. For a modern field commander to lead his troops into action was unheard of, but Elles appreciated the need for the gesture as the stuff of which legends are made; it was an inspired move. The early morning quiet, disturbed only by the slow ticking over of the tank engines, was suddenly broken, just before 6.00 a.m., by the report of a single gun, which set men and machines in motion. At once a short and selective barrage was laid on key areas, as the tanks, in three

33 Spree Farm railhead before the Cambrai battle. Trainloads of Mark IVs, each with a fascine in position, arrive behind ex-Great Western Railway Dean and Armstrong 0-6-0 engines, which were serving with the Railway Operating Department.

34 Mark IV tanks were prominent in the great Battle of Cambrai in November 1917. Ernest, a male tank of 5th Battalion, waits while a wounded crewman is lifted into a Ford 'T' ambulance.

great waves, rolled down on the German defences. Working to a pre-arrranged pattern, successive tanks dropped their fascines into the three main trench lines and pushed on, with the German infantry scattering before them. More tanks followed, including nine that had been specially fitted out with wireless sets to report progress and others equipped with grapnels to clear away areas of barbed wire for the cavalry to pass through. Bringing up the rear were the supply tanks, pulling special sledges loaded with further supplies. There were some reverses. On a ridge near Flesquières sixteen tanks were destroyed as, one by one, they presented themselves as targets to German field batteries. Another tank was lost near Masnières, when it tried to cross a damaged bridge over the L'Escaut Canal, which gently gave way beneath it.

Cambrai was planned as a three-day raid and, at the end

of that time, it could be judged a complete success. However, if it came as a surprise to the Germans, the British High Command was no less overcome. Faced with a breakthrough, the like of which they had never anticipated, they had no reserves available to exploit it. The cavalry made some attempts to push forward but it needed no more than a single undiscovered machine-gun to hold them up and they never got beyond the canal. Anxious to capitalize on success, the surviving tanks with their weary crews and the equally worn out infantry, were exhorted to push on as best they could. By 27 November they had carved out a salient some 11km (7 miles) wide by 9km (6 miles) deep, but German resistance was stiffening. The counter-attack began on the 30th and Haig simply did not have the strength to resist, so a withdrawal was ordered. By 7 December most of the ground so gloriously won was back in German hands. As a victory, Cambrai was short-lived; as a pointer it would last forever but, for the present, it had vindicated the trust of those who had pinned their faith on the tank. It was the harbinger of victory.

Another Victoria Cross, posthumous like the last, was awarded to a member of the Corps. Captain R. W. L. Wain lost his tank and most of his crew during an attack on a German strongpoint. Already wounded, he took one of the Lewis guns and made a single-handed attack on the position, driving out the enemy at the cost of his own life.

35 *Some Mark I female tanks were modified to carry wireless. The sponson was modified to house the set and an aerial was fitted. Her Majesty Queen Mary inspects this one at Erin, the Tank Corps base in France.*

CHAPTER IV
1918, Year of Victory

Cambrai not only restored the credibility of the Tank Corps at Haig's headquarters, it also had a marked effect on its relationship with the infantry. With few exceptions, those who had gone into action alongside tanks never wanted to go without them again. One man who might have expected to reap some benefit from all this was, however, sacrificed instead to political expediency. Albert Stern, whose forthright, but unmilitary ways had upset a number of important people, was removed from his post as head of the Mechanical Warfare Supply Department by the Prime Minister as part of a political deal that enabled Winston Churchill to resume a position of authority as Minister of Munitions. Stern was not lost to the tanks altogether: he was appointed by Churchill as Commissioner for Mechanical Warfare to co-ordinate allied production, a post of some significance now that the United States had joined openly in the Allied cause. It was naturally expected that America, with her vast industrial capacity, would soon be producing tanks on the grand scale but it took longer than anticipated for her to organize that industry on a war footing, so that, in fact, no American-built tanks saw action during the war. Instead the United States Army had to rely on British and French machines to equip her new tank arm. Tank development in Britain had been retarded on two accounts. In the first place the low standing of the tanks generally reduced the priority accorded to them, while the large number of Mark IVs still building monopolized industrial capacity. Plans for a replacement tank, the Mark V, were well advanced and an order for 200 male and 200 female had already been placed with Metropolitan. The basic outline and general layout was much the same as the Mark IV although frontal armour was now increased to 14mm. The most obvious external difference was a raised cab at the rear, similar in size to the driver's cab, which provided better all-round vision and a more secure location from which to attach the unditching beam. This rear cab could indeed serve as a sort of command post, since the tank commander had now been relieved of his responsibility for working the steering brakes by the adoption of the Wilson epicyclic transmission. Behind the rear cab, therefore, was a manually operated semaphore device by means of which, in theory, tank commanders could communicate. In practice this did not often happen since the signalling equipment was usually the first thing to be shot away in action. At the very rear of the hull extra escape hatches were provided, together with a further mounting point for a machine-gun. This was done to discourage enemy soldiers from gathering behind the tank, where on earlier types they had been relatively safe and able to attack the tank if it was halted.

The epicyclic drive, as already explained, placed all control of the tank in one pair of hands. The driver was provided with the basic controls, including a four-speed gear change, along with two levers that operated the brakes on the epicyclic gear. These could be used either to alter the speed of one track, or stop it altogether, depending on how firmly they were pulled and this system also dispensed with the clumsy differential housing that took up so much space in the earlier models. The new transmission was further enhanced by the adoption of a new engine to replace the Daimler. Stern had appreciated the need for this since late 1916 and he had engaged a gifted young engineer, Harry Ricardo, to design it. The demands and limitations imposed upon the designer were daunting in the extreme for it was laid down that the new engine must fit into the same location as the Daimler, that it should develop at least 150hp and that it should operate at extreme angles to the horizontal without burning oil, which could produce tell-tale fumes. Furthermore, because of priorities enforced in favour of aircraft production, neither aluminium nor high tensile steel could be used. Ricardo succeeded to the point that Stern was prepared to order 700 units straight off the drawing-board—causing astonishment at the War Office—and to organize a consortium of small firms to produce them. Like the Daimler, the Ricardo was a straight six-cylinder type and increased capacity was obtained by taking advantage of the extra height available within the tank. Removable panels on the crankcase enabled extensive maintenance to be undertaken without the need to lift the engine out.

Contemporary with the Mark V was another design known as the Mark VI, which, although it was never built, exhibited a number of interesting features which were adopted as a result of combat experience. Sponsons were abandoned in favour of a single six-pounder gun mounted in the nose. This would have allowed the driver to judge the gunner's requirements with greater accuracy and to lay the tank on the firing line. The remainder of the crew were to occupy an elevated central structure, which would have eased internal communication and general effectiveness in battle. In order to leave the centre of the tank clear, the Ricardo engine was positioned to one side and the drive train modified accordingly. The Mark VI was also designed to have 73cm (29in) wide tracks, wider than earlier models, to spread the weight on soft ground. The United States Army placed large orders for the new type but it was considered too radical a departure from current practice, in view of the need for continuous production, and was abandoned at the wooden mock-up stage.

36 *A 16 Battalion Mark V male tank, with some of its crew and mascot. The frame was exactly the same size as the earlier models but it featured a more powerful engine, epicyclic transmission and a rear cab. Notice, too, the semaphore signalling device.*

37 *This female Mark V demonstrates its ability to pass through complicated wire entanglements. It mounts four Hotchkiss machine-guns and displays the white/red/white British recognition markings.*

The little Chaser tank, designed by William Tritton and shown at the Oldbury Trials, was duly developed into the Medium Mark A, or Whippet tank. Fosters built 200 of them and the first examples appeared early in 1918. The tracks were of a lower profile than on the heavy tanks and the superstructure was completely different. The engine compartment was at the front, with an armoured cab for three at the rear. Mountings were provided for up to four Hotchkiss guns, for no male version was planned and it had already been decided to replace the Lewis in all tanks. Tritton appreciated the need for one-man control but chose not to use the Wilson system and pursued a pet idea of his own. This involved the use of two engines, one for each track, and the type chosen was the 45hp Tylor, a four-cylinder model used in London buses. Each engine was coupled, through its own clutch, to a separate four-speed gearbox and bevel drive to the track, so that the driver was faced with a bewildering array of controls. At 14 tons, it was about half the weight of an old Mark I, and twice as fast, having a top speed of 12·9kmph (8mph). In the right hands it was both quick and manoeuvrable, but it took a long time to train a driver, while the need to service two engines instead of one used up a lot of valuable workshop time.

As the momentum of tank production got back into full swing for 1918, new offensives were planned to suit. These were, however, soon overtaken by events when, with the collapse of resistance in Russia, the Germans were able to transfer great numbers of men to the Western Front. With these suitably trained in new battle techniques, based on

38 Medium A tank 'Princess Mary' enjoys a mud bath. The name is painted on the armoured petrol tank cover, behind which is the engine compartment. The fighting cab is at the back.

rapid infiltration rather than massed frontal assault, the first major German offensive in the west since 1914 now began. Launched in mid-March, it aimed to split and decimate the British and French Armies before the Americans arrived to reinforce them, and it very nearly succeeded. By this time the Germans also had some tanks of their own. Most were British machines, mainly Mark IVs, rearmed with German weapons, that had been captured in 1917. They were taken to a German workshop complex at Charleroi in Belgium, refurbished and issued to the troops, who were trained in the same area. Germany also produced a tank of her own, a bulky fortress on tracks known as the A7V, but only about twenty were completed before the end of the war.

British plans for defensive operations with tanks were almost non-existent. Two options seemed to be open: tanks could be held well back, as a strong reserve to be employed as the nucleus of the counter-attack or, following a scheme suggested by General Elles, tanks could be laid up in hidden locations, just behind the British lines, to emerge at an appropriate moment, in order to cut off and isolate groups of attackers. In practice, this tactic of the 'Savage Rabbit', as it came to be known, tended to be wasteful and ineffective. The Mark IV, which still predominated in France, was

39 *The Germans captured large numbers of British tanks during the spring offensive of 1918. These were refurbished at their workshops at Charleroi, Belgium, and used against their former owners. Those shown are mostly Mark IVs; British-built tanks outnumbered the native German design in their service.*

40 *Germany designed the A7V when the success of the British tanks was revealed. Built to a cumbersome design, it only appeared in small numbers and far too late to save the day. This one was captured by British troops at the end of the war.*

altogether too slow for the work, German troops were trained to avoid tanks where they could and, being swifter on foot than a tank, they invariably got away. Probably the most effective contribution made by the Tank Corps in the successful response to the German attack was the provision of the Lewis gun parties, working on foot, but it was a sad waste of highly trained tank crews.

By April it was clear that the German effort had been expended, but they were by no means defeated. Still prepared to try elsewhere, on 24 April, they mounted an attack, supported by tanks, against the British at Villers-Bretonneux on the Somme. It was not the first time that the Germans had used tanks and, it is clear, from their previous experience that entrenched British troops were just as unwilling to face armoured vehicles on the battlefields as their enemy counterparts had been in 1916. The difference, on this occasion, was that there were British tanks nearby, and thus the stage was set for the first battle between opposing tanks. It was less than decisive: the leading A7V damaged two female British machines which left the field, while, in turn, the German tank was disabled by shots from a Mark IV male machine under the command of Lieutenant Frank Mitchell of 1st Battalion. The other German tanks turned away from Mitchell's fire, but he lost his own tank later in the day to enemy artillery.

A short distance away from the scene of Mitchell's action, a group of seven Whippet tanks of 3rd Battalion, under Captain Tommy Price, was lying in wait in a wood. A reconnaissance aircraft, of the newly formed Royal Air Force, dropped a message to the effect that two battalions of German infantry were lurking nearby, and the small group of tanks set out to deal with them. Racing down in line abreast, they cut clean through the surprised German soldiers, reformed and charged again from the other side, accounting for some 400 troops at a cost of one tank and three men of the British force.

It will be noted, from the above, that by this time the identifying letters had been replaced with numbers, since it was anticipated that more battalions would be raised than there would be letters of the alphabet. As it turned out, they were still one letter short at 25 battalions by the time the Armistice was signed, but at the time it was confidently predicted that the war would continue well into 1919. The continued expansion of the Tank Corps, authorized after Cambrai, encountered a set-back in the spring, due to War Office vacillation. Infantry losses, which included 80,000 prisoners, had so alarmed the High Command that even relatively small requirements of the Tank Corps were subject to revision. Likewise the delivery of the new Mark V was affected, since other equipment was accorded priority, although matters were duly resolved, so that, by July, seventeen battalions, brigaded now in groups of three, were in France. Meanwhile the delivery process in Britain had been improved with the opening of a new, central tank-testing ground at Newbury in Berkshire, and by the use of the new train-ferry port at Richborough in Kent.

The early summer months saw three small, but significant, actions supported by the Tank Corps in an effort to try out the strength of German resistance in certain areas. The first took the form of a night attack on 22 June. The risks of using tanks in the dark had been much debated and the results were suprising. A concentrated trench mortar barrage stopped the infantry, but the five female tanks, their engine sound muffled by planes, carried out the raid on their own. Chance encounters with groups of German infantry caused the enemy numerous casualties and all five tanks returned undamaged, despite the fact that one tank was attacked by a mass of soldiers, who had to be fought off with revolvers.

On 4 July, the Mark V went into action for the first time. American and Australian troops were involved, the latter for the first time since Bullecourt in 1917, so the Tank Corps was on its mettle. Sixty tanks of the 13th Battalion took part in this action, the Battle of Hamel, which was a smooth and effective operation. The Mark V was immensely popular at

first; it was quiet and easy to handle while, probably for the first time, there were no pre-battle breakdowns to reduce the numbers. Crews later complained of conditions within the Mark V, since the radiators drew their air from outside the tank instead of from within, so that conditions were particularly difficult to bear. On 23 July, at Moreuil, 9th Battalion supported the French Army. Despite the fact that the infantry and tanks seemed to be fighting separate battles, and tank casualties were fairly high, all objectives were gained and the battalion was awarded the Croix de Guerre by the grateful French.

Plans were now being laid for another large-scale offensive in August, earlier raids having indicated that the German Army was badly shaken. In the meantime another new type of tank arrived in France. The limitations of the fascine and the ineffectiveness of the 'Tadpole Tail' have already been explained but the problem of wider trenches still remained. A lightweight wood and metal structure, called the Crib, was evolved to replace the fascine and Central Workshops also solved the problem of a longer tank. A redundant Mark IV had been taken and cut in half, just behind the sponson, where new panels were inserted to increase the overall length by 1·8m (6ft). The tank thus retained its structural integrity since the hull, between the

41 *Mark V* female tank No. 9766 boarding a Rectank wagon at the Metropolitan works. The wagons were specially designed for carrying tanks; screw jacks acting on the rails at each end supported the weight during loading. The Naval Petty Officer standing alongside is a reminder that the Royal Navy was responsible for testing all new tanks in Britain and delivering them to the Channel ports.*

frames, was longer too, although the extra length of track on the ground made it slightly more difficult to steer. However, it worked well enough for a production version, known as the Mark V* to follow the last Mark V down the line at Birmingham and, in due course, some 600, out of a total order for 700 were completed before the end of the war. As its title suggests, the Mark V* was really little more than a modified Mark V. The new side panels included a door which contained an extra machine-gun mount and the rear cab assembly was reshaped to include sloping front and rear faces, which also had mountings for machine-guns. Most of these tanks also had wider, 66cm (26in), tracks in order to spread the extra weight. These had been considered back in 1916 but, probably for production reasons, had so far not been made. The longer tank included a large space behind the engine and another idea was tried whereby a team of machine-gunners could be transported into action complete

35

with their weapons. The plan was to have them dismount once the enemy trenches had been taken in order that they might establish a strong defensive point in the event of a rapid counter-attack. When it was tried, during the Amiens battle, it was discovered that the infantry were overcome by the conditions inside the tank so that they were in no shape to fight when they got out. By the end of July 1918 a formidable tank force had been assembled in France; nine battalions of heavy tanks, two battalions of Whippets and the 17th Battalion, which had recently been converted to armoured cars with a view to exploiting the expected breakthrough.

At 4.00 a.m. on 8 August the first elements of this force rolled forward on a 21km (13 mile) wide front. The early morning mist was so thick that tanks steered on a compass course, but it also hid them from the German sentries, whose first intimation of the attack arrived in the shape of a furious barrage, which fell on their trenches a few minutes before the tanks appeared. The Whippets had been instructed to work with the cavalry and this resulted in a sort of hare and tortoise race. The tanks could not keep up with the mounted arm on good going but they soon outstripped the latter when enemy machine-guns were located. Lieutenant C. B. Arnold, commanding the 6th Battalion

42 The Mark V was followed in production by the Mark V*, which was longer to cope with wider trenches. This tank was somewhat underpowered – it used the same engine as the Mark V – and was difficult to steer on account of the greater length.

43 A Mark V* male tank boarding a train from the loading ramp at Central Workshops. The locomotive is an American built Baldwin saddle tank.

Whippet 'Musical Box', went on a ten-hour rampage in German territory before the tank was knocked out by a field gun and the crew captured. The Austin armoured cars were drawn across the rough ground by tanks and then released on the main road to St Quentin, where they caused havoc, shooting up columns of troops and transport and over running a German Corps Headquarters at Framerville.

Tank losses were severe; since Cambrai the Germans had perfected the technique of using field artillery for anti-tank work and when a slow moving heavy tank was caught in the open, it was often successfully knocked out. By noon many of the main objectives were in British hands. The diminishing number of serviceable tanks, coupled with increased German resistance, slowed down the offensive over the next few days but the damage had been done. It was now clear at the highest level in Germany that the war was effectively lost; the low morale of the front-line troops had finally permeated to the top.

44 The breakout from Amiens restored mobility away from the trench zones. Once again the armoured car found a place in the order of battle and 17th Battalion, Tank Corps, was equipped with twin-turreted Austins. The cars were towed over the trench system by tanks and released to wreak havoc behind the German lines. The cars ultimately led the Tank Corps into Germany and the circle was complete.

On 21 August, the battle resumed but not where the Germans were expecting it. With their reserves massed to resist a follow up over the same ground, they were thrown off balance by an attack in a more northerly sector. Day after day the blow fell in a different area so that enemy reserves could never be in the right place at the right time and on the 26th Ludendorf ordered a general withdrawal to the

46 A female Mark V crashes through a road block. It carries some small brushwood fascines and two infantry trench bridges.

45 'Musical Box', of 6th Battalion, commanded by Lieutenant Arnold, fought a private war for ten hours before being knocked out, far behind the German lines. This was on 8 August 1918, the first day of the battle of Amiens. Some months later British troops came across the abandoned tank and used it to shelter wounded prisoners.

Hindenburg Line. Tank stocks were getting lower but the arrival of the 16th Battalion and the American 301st stabilized the situation for a while. The 301st was the only United States unit to be equipped with British heavy tanks—Mark V*—so on this account it was trained and brigaded with the British Tank Corps.

Victoria Crosses were awarded, posthumously, to Lieutenant C. H. Sewell, who had sacrificed his life rescuing the crew of another Whippet who had become trapped, and to Lieutenant-Colonel R. A. West, who had led his men on horseback in the face of concentrated enemy fire.

The attack on the Hindenburg Line began on 27 September. The British sector lying between Arras and St Quentin included that celebrated objective of the year before, Cambrai. In the belief that the Canal du Nord, which entwines with the Hindenburg Line in this region, would be an impassable obstacle to tanks, it was decided to dig out some old Mark Is from Central Workshops, to have them stiffened internally with heavy timbers, and for them to be driven into the canal at a suitable point to form a causeway for the fighting tanks. Every one of them broke down during the approach march but, as it turned out, other tanks had no difficulty getting across so the Mark Is were not missed. An 8km (5 mile) gap was smashed through the German defences, followed on 5 October by the breaching of the Hindenburg Support Line, the last effective fortified barrier this side of Germany. Now at last the war was carried into open country once again and on the 8th a fairly large-scale tank battle developed, at least by First World War standards, when eleven German tanks were engaged by 12th Battalion and six destroyed. The majority of the enemy machines were captured British Mark IVs rearmed with German weapons.

The fighting was to continue for another month and the surviving British tanks were stretched to the limit. Forty-eight tanks were available for the crossing of the Selle River on 17 October and thirty-seven were scraped together for a push towards Mons on 4 November. On the following day a mere eight Whippets of 6th Battalion took part in the last tank action of the war, beyond the Mormal forest. The final honour fell to the 17th Battalion, who entered Germany in their armoured cars on 1 December and bore the Tank Corps flag into Cologne on the 6th.

In Britain 1918 was marked not just by an upsurge in tank production but by an amazing rash of new designs. They appeared in bewildering numbers at a remarkable pace but only a few entered production and none of them got to France in time to see action. Priority seems to have been given to the medium tank designs. No doubt this was partly because the original Whippet, essentially a 1916 model, was ripe for improvement but it was also because of an appreciation of the need for faster tanks, suitable for exploitation. The situation was complicated by the appearance of two rival designs, for at this stage Wilson and Tritton seem to have gone their separate ways. Walter Wilson's offering was the Medium B, which outwardly resembled a scaled-down heavy tank in its hull outline. It was powered by a shortened four cylinder version of the Ricardo engine, driving through a Mark V style transmission. The main crew compartment was at the front, where an enlarged superstructure contained mountings for four Hotchkiss guns with two more in small sponson-shaped doors in the track frames. It was both heavier and slower than the Medium A and no better protected but it was much easier to drive. However, the main drawback would seem to have been the cramped engine compartment, which made maintenance very difficult, yet orders were placed for 450 of which some 48 were completed. William Tritton produced the Medium C, or Hornet, which was a larger machine altogether, powered by a full six-cylinder Ricardo engine. Once again the Wilson transmission system was chosen and the layout was not unlike the Medium B. It was a roomy tank with a trench-crossing ability equal to a heavy tank of the Mark IV type and with the same armour protection. The tank had stations for five Hotchkiss guns in the superstructure, although only four were carried, a raised commander's lookout and provision for mounting an anti-aircraft gun. The performance was exceptional and it was

47 Mark V tanks of 8th Battalion pause during the final advance to the Hindenburg Line. Each tank carries a crib, a trench-crossing aid that replaced the fascine. In the foreground German prisoners supply some interest for a group of Allied soldiers.

48 A female Mark IV escorts captured Germans with a stretcher through the ruined banks of the Canal du Nord. Notice the extra petrol cans in the rear stowage tray.

49 *Walter Wilson designed the Medium B as a replacement for the Whippet. In spite of the undoubted genius of its designer, this tank failed to come up to expectations, although it saw action in Russia in 1919. This example was built in Glasgow from funds subscribed by the citizens of Newcastle.*

50 *The Medium C was William Tritton's design and was considered to be the best tank of the war, although it never saw action. For the first time, in a British tank, the engine compartment was separated from the crew area. This one has been equipped with a wireless set although it still retains the semaphore device.*

very popular with the troops, although only about 45 were completed, mostly by Fosters. It was chosen as one of the two types, the other being the Mark V, to equip the post-war Tank Corps. A male version, mounting the old, long six-pounder gun, was projected but never built and it is interesting that, in 1918, this was being referred to in very modern terminology, as a tank destroyer.

Despite the obvious success and general popularity of the Wilson transmission system there were always those who thought they could improve upon it. Even 20 Squadron made an attempt, converting an old Mark II into a one-man-drive tank by fitting a Lanchester epicyclic gearbox, which had the distinct advantage of allowing gears to be changed on the move. The major contender, however, came in the form of the Williams-Janney hydraulic system, which had been rejected at Oldbury. In theory it was an ideal system, since it offered infinitely variable speed control without the need to change gear or operate a clutch. Special adjustable pumps, operated by the engine, transmitted drive to the track sprockets and the action of these pumps was controlled by a pair of handwheels in the cab. The system reappeared in 1918 in the Mark VII design, three of which were built by Brown Brothers in Edinburgh. Outwardly the tanks looked like longer Mark Vs but they are instantly recognizable by the profusion of extra cooling louvres along the top of the hull. This indicates at once that the old problem of cooling the oil had still not been solved and no production followed, although the system was tried on a number of other occasions after the war, always with the same result.

Although they saw considerable service in the last months of the war, the lengthened Mark V★ tanks suffered from all the vices inherent in what was, after all, a glorified field modification. A much improved version known as the Mark V★★ was just about to enter service when the war ended and this solved all the problems, since it was designed as a longer tank in its own right. The difference was most noticeable at the rear, where the track frames ended in a much steeper angle, but the interior layout was also altered. The engine, an uprated 225hp version of the Ricardo, was situated somewhat further back, leaving the front end clear for the crew, and the two separate cabs were combined into one composite structure at the front. It was heavier than the Mark V★ and gave about the same performance but it was much easier to handle and well liked by the crews. Only about twenty-five were built, none of which saw action, but it made a most important contribution to tank development in another sphere. At least two of the tanks were supplied to the Royal Engineers, who converted them at the Experimental Bridging Establishment at Christchurch, into tank bridgelayers. The second tank carried a powerful hydraulic pump, which actuated a multi-purpose jib that could be used as a field crane, bridgelayer, demolition-charge placer or mine sweeper. This latter role had been tried once before, although never developed, when a Mark IV was converted, by the addition of heavy rollers on beams mounted ahead of the tracks, to explode mines. The interesting point is that the need for an armoured engineer vehicle was appreciated at such an early stage in tank

51 Three Mark VIIs were built by Brown Bros of Edinburgh. They featured the hydraulic Williams-Janney transmission again but suffered from the same overheating problems and were never used in action. The hull design was a compromise between the original shape and the Tadpole Tail.

52 A very muddy Mark V★★ male tank with a group of VIPs and the inevitable dog. The gun has been run back on its trunnions and the revised shape of the superstructure is visible.

53 A Mark V★★ was adapted as a universal engineers tank with a hydraulic crane attachment, shown here lifting the rear end of a Foster-Daimler tractor.

development. The practice died out completely between the wars and was not resurrected until about 1942, without, it seems, any reference to this pioneering work.

Albert Stern's new post as Commissioner for Allied Tank Development bore fruit in 1918, with the appearance of the Mark VIII, which was a combined Anglo-American design. Known also as the International, it was the longest and heaviest tank of all, powered by a V12 engine, driving through a special two-speed epicyclic, without the benefit of primary gears. Maximum armour thickness was 16mm and the engine was contained in a separate compartment at the rear. The superstructure had some features in common with the abandoned Mark VI design, with a raised lookout for the commander. Only a male version was planned, with the six-pounders mounted in new-style sponsons of American design, while the secondary armament was increased to seven machine-guns, Hotchkiss in the British and Brownings in the American version. A huge tank factory was being built in France, since all the Allied armies were supposed to use the new tank. As with many other designs, the Mark VIII was completed too late to see service. Britain built a few, powered by a Ricardo V12 engine, and one of these was supplied to the United States. After the war the Americans built 100, powered by their Liberty V12 aero engine. In 1940, these tanks, along with the American version of the French Renault, were actually supplied to Canada for training purposes.

The ultimate wartime design was the Mark IX, which was not really a tank at all; today it would be described as an armoured personnel carrier. One of its functions was as a supply carrier, to replace the motley collection of converted gun tanks then in use. Its other role almost brought the wartime design trend full circle, round again to Crompton's original idea for a landship to carry a trench-storming party. It is now fully appreciated that the tank and armoured troop-carrier are complementary, not rival, types but, like many conclusions reached in the First World War, it went out of fashion soon afterwards. The Mark IX was designed to transport either 10 tons of stores or thirty fully equipped soldiers under armour. Almost everything about the design was subordinate to this purpose. The hull was almost

54 The equipment of the Mark V** could be used for a variety of roles, including mine-sweeping, demolition placement and bridge laying, as shown here.

55 The Mark VIII, or International, was the ultimate manifestation of British heavy-tank design during the war. An early model is seen here inside the North British Locomotive Company works in Glasgow.

56 One Mark VIII went to America for trials and in due course 100 tanks of the same type were built there.

57 A Mark IX troop-carrier, showing the large doors in the sides. The louvred panel at the front reveals the new location of the engine, which kept the main hull area clear. Extra stores could be carried in a tray on top of the hull.

rectangular, with a slightly upturned nose and steeply sloped rear. Four large oval doors were provided, two on each side, for easy access, and the interior was drastically rearranged to suit. The engine, a Ricardo straight six, was moved to the front, along with the radiator. All the control rods, except the main drive shaft, were installed beneath the roof. Nothing could be done about the drive shaft, which ran the full length of the floor, but the rear end was only slightly encumbered by the bevel box and cross shaft. Stout cross members were located at intervals along the bottom of the hull to provide the structural integrity that would otherwise have been compromised by the almost total absence of the internal track frames. A useful minor addition was a drinking-water tank for the passengers. The cab roof was fitted with a raised look-out, and the silencer was directly behind the cab, leaving the rest of the roof free to serve as an extra load-carrying space, while brackets were fitted for sledge towing. There were no sponsons and the fixed armament was limited to a couple of Hotchkiss machine-guns, mountings for which were provided at the front and rear. A series of loopholes, with protected covers, was arranged down both sides and through which the infantry passengers could fire their rifles, should the need arise. About 36 Mark IXs were completed, but only one, in addition to the prototype, was ready before the end of hostilities. This was sent out to France, just before the Armistice, equipped as an armoured ambulance. The prototype was used for another experiment, which actually took place at Hendon on Armistice Day. The tank was modified by the addition of a large, raised conning tower and a series of air-filled drums along each side and across the front. Thus equipped, with doors suitably sealed, it launched itself upon the Welsh Harp reservoir, and floated about for a while propelled in the water by large paddles connected to the track plates. This was probably the first attempt on record to make a tank amphibious.

A number of other designs were in the air at the end of the war but only one had reached the mock-up stage. This was a replacement for the original gun carrier. It was similar in outline to a conventional Mark V tank, but the rear end was open and reshaped to permit the loading and transporting of a field gun. It would appear that the weapon in question was the 18-pounder or the 4·5 inch howitzer. Either was far more suited to the mobile role than the bigger guns used on the first model. In this case there is no evidence to suggest that the gun would have been fired from the carrier, since it was facing the wrong way, but, unfortunately, this interesting design was never built.

With the ending of hostilities the strength of the British Army was steadily run down. The Tank Corps was no exception but there was a chance that it might be disbanded altogether. Reactionary elements within the Army saw it as a transient phenomenon, a specific antidote to a specific problem, which, if they had anything to do with it, would never occur again. In the meantime a force, composed largely of Mark Vs, was retained in Germany as part of the army of occupation, while three special detachments were organized and despatched to Russia in a vain effort to stem the Bolshevik uprisings. Medium A and B tanks, along with Mark Vs, were used by these detachments but it was a losing battle and the survivors were withdrawn by 1920.

Civil unrest in Ireland and the threat of serious strikes in Britain also kept a small tank force occupied in each country for a time, but this kind of work was better suited to the armoured cars, which now came under the control of the Corps and also saw action in various trouble spots around the Middle East. The long term future was not decided until 1922, when it was agreed that the Tank Corps should be retained as a separate body, and this was further strengthened in 1923 when the Royal accolade was granted.

58 The prototype Mark IX was tested, on Armistice Day 1918, as an amphibian with large air drums attached to the hull. Movement in the water was by paddles fitted to the tracks.

Once the position in Europe had stabilized, the vast number of tanks remaining in France were gradually brought home to Bovington, where they lay, in sad rusting lines, on the heathland to the north of the camp. In 1919, a branch line had been laid to the camp from Wool station, on the London and South Western Railway, largely with the aid of prisoners-of-war, and this soon saw a modest two-way traffic when selected Mark IV machines, almost all females, were despatched to various towns that had raised appreciable sums of money during War Bond drives. The tank would arrive at the local station, complete with its crew, who would then drive it to the chosen location and disable it, by removing the driving chains, while appropriate speeches were made. As these tanks lacked both guns and means of motion, it was felt that they could not be used by disaffected groups bent on revolution. The sole survivor of these presentation tanks still remains at Ashford in Kent.

Two tanks had a most unusual fate: they were purchased by a syndicate of retired officers and fitted with a passenger deck above the hull. They spent some time giving rides to the public at Southend-on-Sea. Their less fortunate companions went to the scrap heap, all that is except a select few which were fenced off at Bovington and retained for preservation.

60 *The northern end of the line was close to the site of the present workshops and it was from here that many tanks were despatched, after the war, to towns and cities throughout the country. On arrival they were driven to their last resting place and de-activated by the crew, to serve as static war memorials.*

61 *An undignified end for an old war horse; the Mark IV female was operated by a consortium of ex-Tank Corps officers at Southend-on-Sea, where it earned a precarious living with paying passengers on the upper deck.*

59 *The Bovington Camp Railway was completed in 1919. It connected with the London and South Western Railway at Wool, and came into its own when the tanks came home from France. It was operated by the L.S.W.R. and a typical train is seen from across the Frome, headed by an 0-6-0 saddle tank.*

62 *Philip Johnson's modified Medium A, showing the brackets for the road springs, the enlarged engine compartment to contain the Rolls-Royce engine and the bearings for the Mark V epicyclics at the rear. This machine managed a top speed of 48 kmph (30 mph) on trials.*

63 *Following his return to Britain, Johnson devised a revolutionary new type of suspension using wire rope and pulleys and a new type of laterally flexible, monorail track employing the same medium. A Mark V tank was converted by Fowlers of Leeds to test the new system for the proposed Medium D series.*

CHAPTER V
1919, Curtain Call

The sudden collapse of Germany was a surprise to both sides. The Allied High Command had every expectation of the fighting lasting well into 1919 and at Tank Corps Headquarters in France Lieutenant-Colonel J. F. C. Fuller was putting the finishing touches to his own dream of victory. Taking advantage of the renaissance of the tank, Fuller produced what he called his 'Plan 1919'. He proposed making mobility, rather than the power of frontal assault the key to armoured battle. He envisaged a strong force of heavy tanks transfixing the opposition at the front while fast-moving medium tanks would sweep around the flanks and make directly for previously identified command centres where, in Fuller's view, the brains of the armies resided. Once these were destroyed, the fighting limbs would wither from want of direction from above and the entire enemy force would collapse. That, at least, was the idea, but it was just so much wishful thinking without a suitably fast medium tank to carry it out. Although he lacked the engineering skills to make it a reality, Fuller knew where they could be found and, in the meantime, he called his imaginary tank the Medium D.

The man Fuller chose to design his tank was Major Philip Johnson, the officer in charge of No. 3 Advanced Workshop, a special experimental unit based at Erin. Johnson was a gifted and experienced engineer who had been with the Tank Corps almost from its formation. He had been involved in the technical preparation for the Hush Operation and was the brain behind a number of other innovations, but his main interest lay in the business of tank suspensions. Although, as we have seen, none of the British tanks designed during the war had any sort of springing at all, this was not a severe handicap since speed in action was never much more than 3 to 5km (2 or 3 miles) an hour. Some crews could, however, testify to the improved ride that was evident whenever a tank forced its way across a cushion of barbed wire. Certainly if greater speed was required, then some sort of springing was necessary and the first step towards this came in 1917 when, at Johnson's direction, Central Workshops fitted springs to a Mark IV. This was followed by a Medium A which had leaf springs mounted within the frames, and later, a Rolls-Royce engine and Wilson transmission in place of the twin-engine arrangement. In this form the tank put up an amazing performance with a top speed of 48kmph (30mph), and no doubt, for the purpose Fuller had in mind, it would have done perfectly well. It did not satisfy Johnson's desire to revolutionize tank design so he managed to arrange for a transfer to Britain, where, with comprehensive industrial facilities at his disposal, he planned to do even better.

In the summer of 1918, Johnson, now a Lieutenant-Colonel, returned to Britain to work with his old firm, John Fowler and Co. of Leeds. A Mark V tank was supplied as a test bed and, in order to reduce the weight, the sponsons and many other non-essential hull plates were removed, as were the tracks and rollers. Johnson's theories on tank suspension were based on the tensile properties of flexible steel wire rope, the sort of material Fowlers used for their big steam ploughs. Johnson sought to use this instead of springs, partly on the premise that fitting individual springs to each set of rollers increased weight without offering adequate deflection. His plan was to stretch the rope between springs at either end of the tank and thread it alternately over pulleys attached to the track rollers and under pulleys mounted on the hull. By this device the weight of the tank rested on the cable, which in turn rested on the track rollers and, by definition, on the track itself. If the tank encountered a small obstacle in its path, the sets of rollers lifted over it in succession, pushing against the rope and the whole suspension system undulated without affecting the tank itself. In theory it was brilliant, but in practice it was testing the very limits of available technology in materials and it had one great flaw. If a cable parted the entire suspension on that side of the tank was liable to collapse, rendering it helpless at a stroke. Johnson was not deterred, for by this time the war was over and the urgency had gone, so he was free to give more time to his work. He applied equally unorthodox principles to track design. Steering a conventional heavy tank absorbed a great deal of power in the side thrust exerted on the stationary track. What Johnson wanted was a track that would form itself into a curve as the tank turned and to this end he designed a new type which also relied upon a core of wire rope. The shoes were formed from narrow channels of pressed steel, with wooden inserts to reduce wear. Each shoe was free to flex laterally so that it would conform to an irregular ground surface or a turning motion. When it emerged from Fowler's works in the spring of 1919, the Mark V looked more like a wreck than the prototype of a new generation of tanks but it put up an impressive performance during a demonstration in Roundhay Park, Leeds. The only drawback was an unfortunate tendency to throw off the wooden track inserts which, perversely, seemed always to fly in the direction of the distinguished audience.

The new tank that was to run on this novel suspension was

the Medium D. A series of prototypes were built by Fowlers and Wolseley Motors. These were long, low tanks with the fighting compartment at the front, powered by modified aircraft engines. The design specifications required them to be fully amphibious as well but, in the case of the first models, they were found to be too narrow to be stable in the water. A series of improved Medium Ds appeared over the next three years, before Johnson's department was closed down, but these are outside the scope of this book.

The Royal Commission on Awards to Inventors met in 1919 to decide who had invented the tank. The transcript of their proceedings makes interesting reading. Claims were pressed by just about everyone who had anything to do with the origins of the tank and by quite a few who did not. Witness was called from Winston Churchill downwards. Colonel Crompton was supported by his partner, Legros, but denied by his emissary to the United States, George Field. Nesfield and MacFie continued their prize row while a number of claimants who held the King's commission were told that they were only doing their duty and were therefore ineligible for a reward. The evidence in favour of Tritton and Wilson was irrefutable and, with the benefit of hindsight, it is difficult to see how it could be judged otherwise. That they did not so much invent as perfect the weapon is a minor point when compared with their achievement; the lion's share of the reward was thus well directed. Both Stern and Tritton received knighthoods, although Wilson did not. It is pleasing to record that the unhonoured prophet Lancelot de Mole was finally recognized, at least for what might have been.

The question of who gave the tank its name seems as contentious as that of who invented it. Again numerous candidates have been put forward, the preferred being Sir Albert Stern. As the first machines were being completed the need for secrecy was paramount. It was thus felt that a less descriptive title than 'landship' should be found, although it still had to relate to the vehicle's style of construction. It was decided to imply that this invention was a species of mobile water carrier for use in Mesopotamia, so the term 'water carrier' was suggested. This would be perpetuated in the title Water Carrier Committee being applied to the guiding body. Stern, bearing in mind the War Office penchant for initials, decided that he did not relish being known as the secretary of the W.C. Committee. He quickly cast about for an alternative and, fortunately for posterity, 'cistern' was rejected in favour of 'tank'.

By the time the first tanks were ready to leave Foster's works, the Mesopotamia deceit had been dropped and an

64 One of the prototype Medium D high-speed tanks nearing completion at the Wolseley Motors factory in Birmingham.

alternative disguise adopted. This took the form of an inscription, painted on the hull in Russian characters, which in translation read, 'With care to Petrograd'. The value of this ploy is hard to judge since, if taken as a delivery instruction, the phrase would be meaningless to the average Briton or even a moderately well-educated spy. Despite this there is evidence to show that some tanks retained the markings long enough to bear them in action. The entire subject of tank markings is too complicated to compress into a short space but some may be mentioned. The basic colour of the tanks passed from a factory finish of plain grey, on the early models, to the colourful Solomon camouflage and finally to an overall medium brown. When a tank was built it was issued with a number, of three, four or five digits and, in the case of the Whippets, prefixed by the letter A. Tanks issued to battalions had a company identification, which took the form of an initial letter of that battalion and a number to show its place within the company structure. Often the crew chose a name that was generally, although not always, in alphabetical sequence with the battalion. Tanks used for training carried a large two or three-digit number painted on the forward end of the hull. Once the Germans started using captured British tanks, a new device was adopted to distinguish friend from foe. It took the form of red and white bars, painted on both horizontal and vertical faces, normally at the front. The word 'supply' was painted in large white letters on the sponsons of tanks relegated to that role; this was probably done to prevent infantry, in the heat of battle, mistaking them for fighting tanks, and asking for their help. There is, however, one case on record of a couple of supply tanks indulging in an improvised attack and succeeding. The proscribed letters 'W.C.' seen on the back of some tanks at Cambrai, indicated that these were the special wire cutters which the cavalry should follow.

Perhaps, in the end, it is fitting to ask just what contribution the tanks made to victory in 1918. No mechanical aid could be a substitute for the enduring courage of the Allied infantry. However, it remains a fact that, from Cambrai onwards, a series of massive and successful assaults were made, upon increasingly well-defended enemy lines, which showed hitherto unequalled gains for substantially smaller losses, and it was precisely these actions in which the tanks were used, and used properly. The tanks were an uncompromising statement of the will to win, which heartened those who worked with them and dismayed their foes. Had it not been for the tank, it is almost certain that the war would have dragged on, at least into 1919.

65 Tanks could be contrary too; this Mark V crashed through the parapet at the southern end of Wool Bridge, which in those days was the main road to Dorchester. The site is much the same today; Woolbridge Manor is famous for its association with Tess of the D'Urbevilles.

TABLE OF TANK DETAILS

Type Heavy Tanks	Weight tons	Length	Width	Height	Engine B.h.p./r.p.m.	Transmission	Track width inches	Maximum designed top gear speed m.p.h.	Petrol capacity gallons	Radius of Action, miles	Trench crossing capacity	Armament Main	M.G.'s	Ammunition Main	S.A.A.	Armour plate Max./Min. thickness in mm.	Crew
Mks. I–III Male	28	32' 6" with tail	13' 9"	8'	Daimler 6-cylinder 105/1000	Two-speed main gear-box, worm drive and differential with two secondary gear-boxes on differential output shafts. Chain drive to sprocket reduction gear.	20½	3·7	50	23·6	11' 6' with tail 10' without tail	2 × 6-pdr. 40 calibre	4	332	6272	10/6	8
Female	27	26' 5" without tail	13' 9"	8'								—	5	—	30080		
Mark IV Male	28	26' 5"	13' 6"	8' 2"	Daimler 6-cylinder 105/1000	As for Marks I–III.	20½	3·7	70	35	10'	2 × 6-pdr. 23 calibre	4	332	6272	12/6	8
Female	26	26' 5"	10' 6"	8' 2"								—	6	—	30080		
Mark V Male	29	26' 5"	13' 6"	8' 8"	Ricardo 6-cylinder 150/1250	Four-speed gear-box fwd, and reverse bevel box. Epicyclic gears on output shafts thence chain reduction gear	First 200 26½ then 20½	4·6	93	45	10'	2 × 6-pdr. 23 calibre	4	207	5700	12/6	8
Female	28	26' 5"	10' 6"	8' 8"								—	6	—	14100		
Mark V* Male	33	32' 5"	13' 6"	8' 8"	Ricardo 6-cylinder 150/1250	As for Mark V but with lengthened carden shaft.	26½, 20½	4·6	93	40	13'	2 × 6-pdr. 23 calibre	4	207	7800	12/6	8
Female	32	32' 5"	10' 6"	8' 8"								—	6	—	16200		
Mark V** Male	35	32' 5"	12' 10"	9'	Ricardo 6-cylinder 225/1250	As for Mark V but with chain drive inside hull to reduction gear on sprocket hub.	26½	4·6	200	67	13'	2 × 6-pdr. 23 calibre	4	220	6600	12/6	8
Female	34	32' 5"	10' 6"	9'								—	6	—	16200		
Mark VI (Projected)	33	26' 7"	10' 6"	9'	Ricardo 6-cylinder 150/1250	To obtain crew room the engine was to have been displaced to the side. Remainder of transmission as for Mk V.	29½	3·9	120	45	10'	1 × 6-pdr. 23 calibre	4	130	10000	14/6	8
Mark VII	33	29' 10"	13' 9"	8' 7"	Ricardo 6-cylinder 150/1250	Williams-Janney hydraulic variable speed gears, one to each track. Chain drive from reduction gear direct to driving sprocket.	26½	4·25	100	50	10'	2 × 6-pdr. 23 calibre	4	207	7800	12/6	8
Mark VIII	37	34' 2½"	12' 4"	10' 3"	Ricardo V12 or Liberty V12 300/1250	Bevel drive with two-speed epicyclic gears on each output shaft. Chain drive to roller pinion meshing with driving sprocket.	26½	1·4 and 5·25 (on the two epicyclic gear ratios).	200	55	14'	2 × 6-pdr. 23 calibre	7	208	13484	16/6	8

Type	Weight tons	Length	Width	Height	Engine B.h.p./r.p.m.	Transmission	Track width inches	Maximum designed top gear speed m.p.h.	Petrol capacity gallons	Radius of Action, miles	Trench crossing capacity	Armament Main	M.G.'s	Ammunition Main	S.A.A.	Armour plate Max./Min. thickness in mm.	Crew
Medium Tanks																	
Mark A (Whippet)	14	20'	8' 7"	9'	2 × 4-cylinder 45 h.p. Tylor engines. 90 (total)/1250	One engine per track with separate cone clutch, four-speed gear-box and bevel drive to cross shafts, which could be locked.	20½	8·3	70	80	7'	—	4	—	5400	14/6	3
Mark B	18	22' 9"	9' 3"	8' 4"	Ricardo 4-cylinder 100/1250	Four-speed gear-box with bevel box giving forward and reverse. Epicyclic gears on each output shaft. Chain drives direct to driving sprocket.	22½	6·1	85	65	8' 6"	—	4	—	7500	14/6	4
Mark C	20	25' 10"	8' 10½"	9' 7½"	Ricardo 6-cylinder 150/1250	Engine at rear driving forward to four-speed gear-box, bevel box with epicyclics on output shafts. Two-stage chain drive to driving sprocket.	20½	7·9	150	120	10'	—	4	—	7200	12/6	4
Mark D	20	30'	7' 5"	9' 2½"	Siddeley Puma 240/2000	—	20½	25	200	200	12'	—	3	—	—	—	4
Support Tanks																	
Gun Carrier Mark I	27 tare 34 with gun	29' 9" 35' 5" with tail 43' with tail & gun.	11'	9' 4"	Daimler 6-cylinder 105/1000	Engine at rear— forward to two-speed gear-box and worm drive with differential. Two-speed secondary gear-boxes on output shafts. Chain drive to pinion meshing with driving sprocket.	20½	3·7	80	35	12'	1 × 60-pdr. or 6" Howitzer	1	120	2000	8/8	5
Salvage Tank		As for Gun Carrier.				—	—	—	—	—	—	—	—	—	—	—	—
Mark IX	27 tare 37 loaded	31' 11"	8' 1"	8' 8"	Ricardo 6-cylinder 150/1250	Four-speed gear-box bevel box and epicyclic gears. Chain drive to driving sprockets. Engine very far forward with long carden shaft to gear-box at back of tank.	20½	3·35	100	42	12' 6"	—	1	—	1800	10/6	4

General arrangement of Machine Mark IV

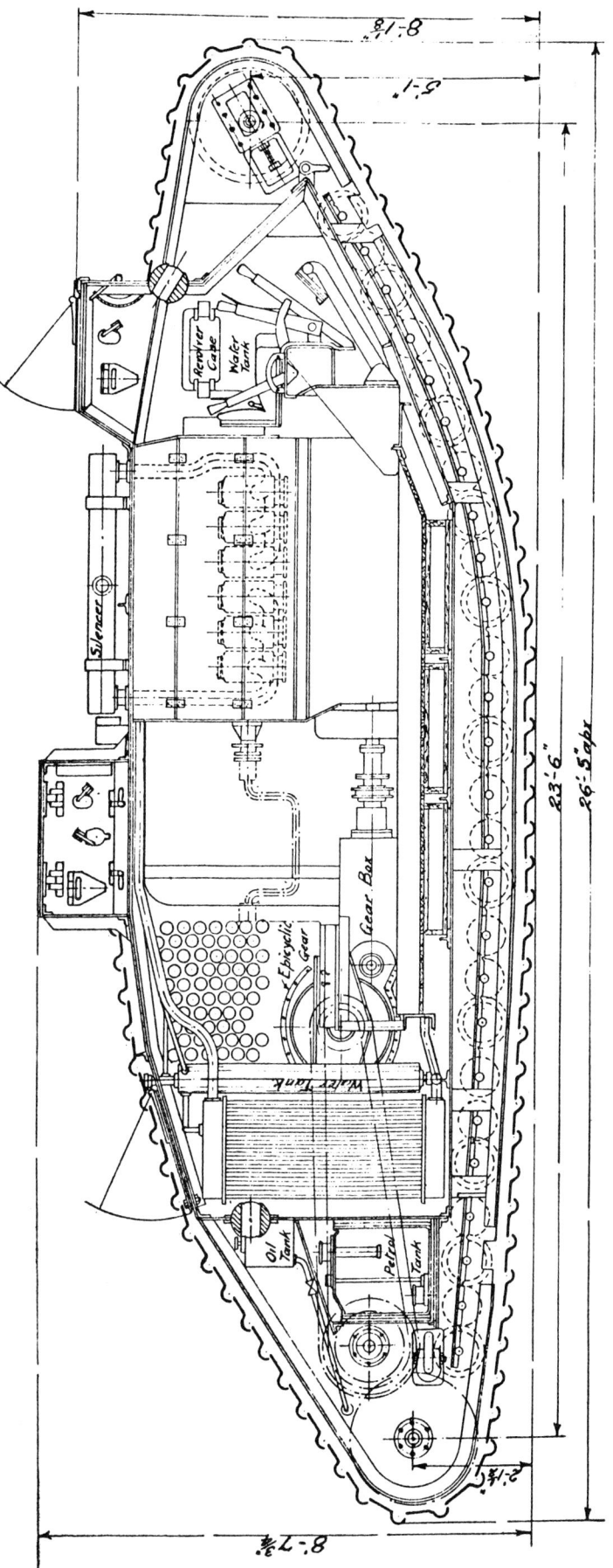

General arrangement of Machine Mark V

General arrangement of Machine Mark V*

SECTIONAL ELEVATION.

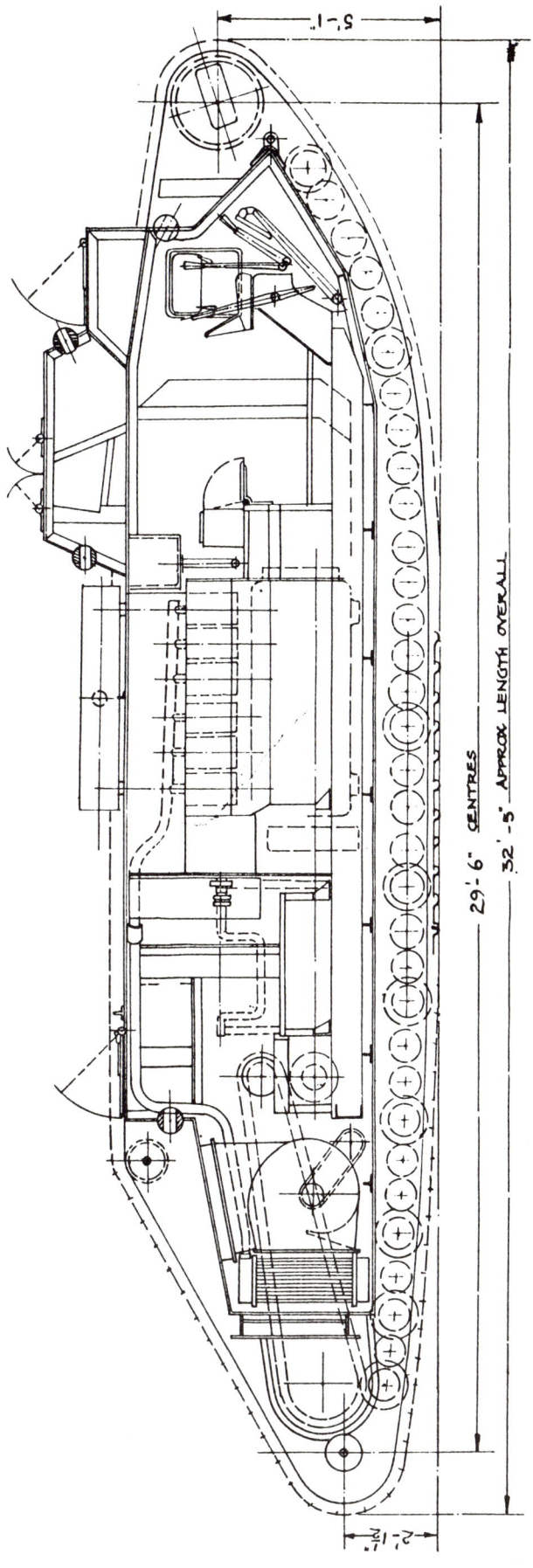

SECTIONAL ELEVATION

General arrangement of Machine Mark V**

General arrangement of Machine Mark VII

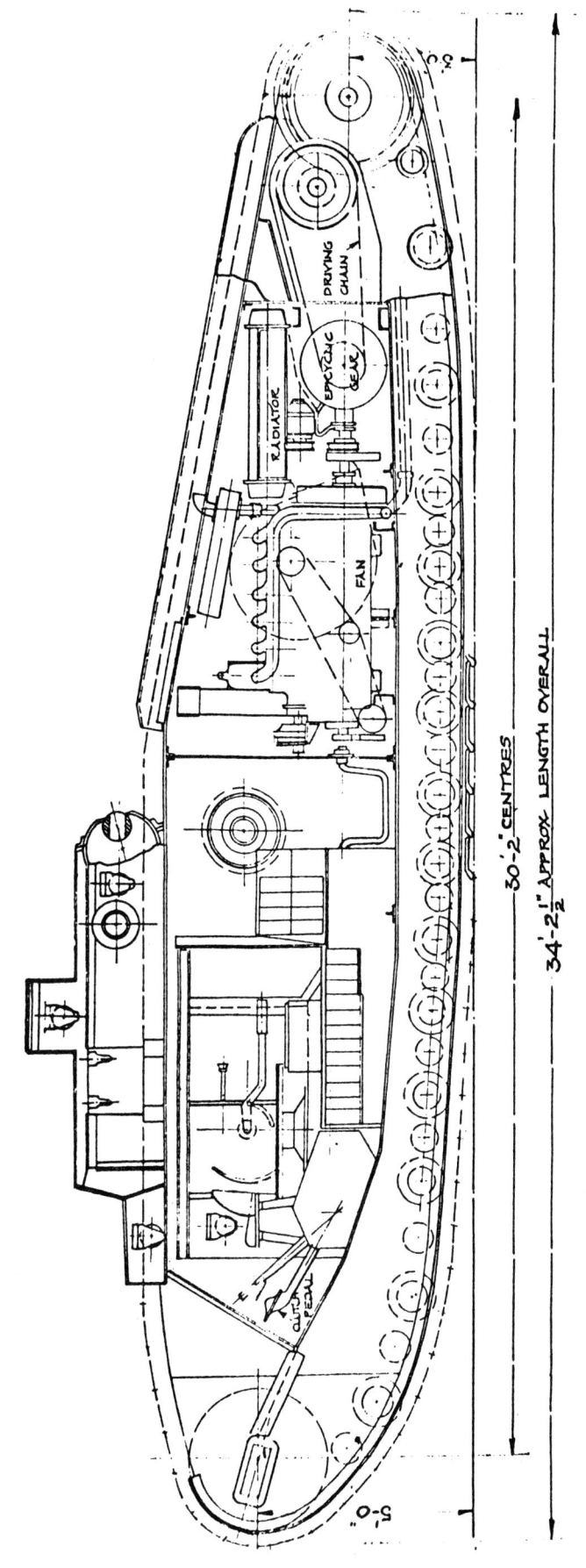

General arrangement of Machine Mark VIII

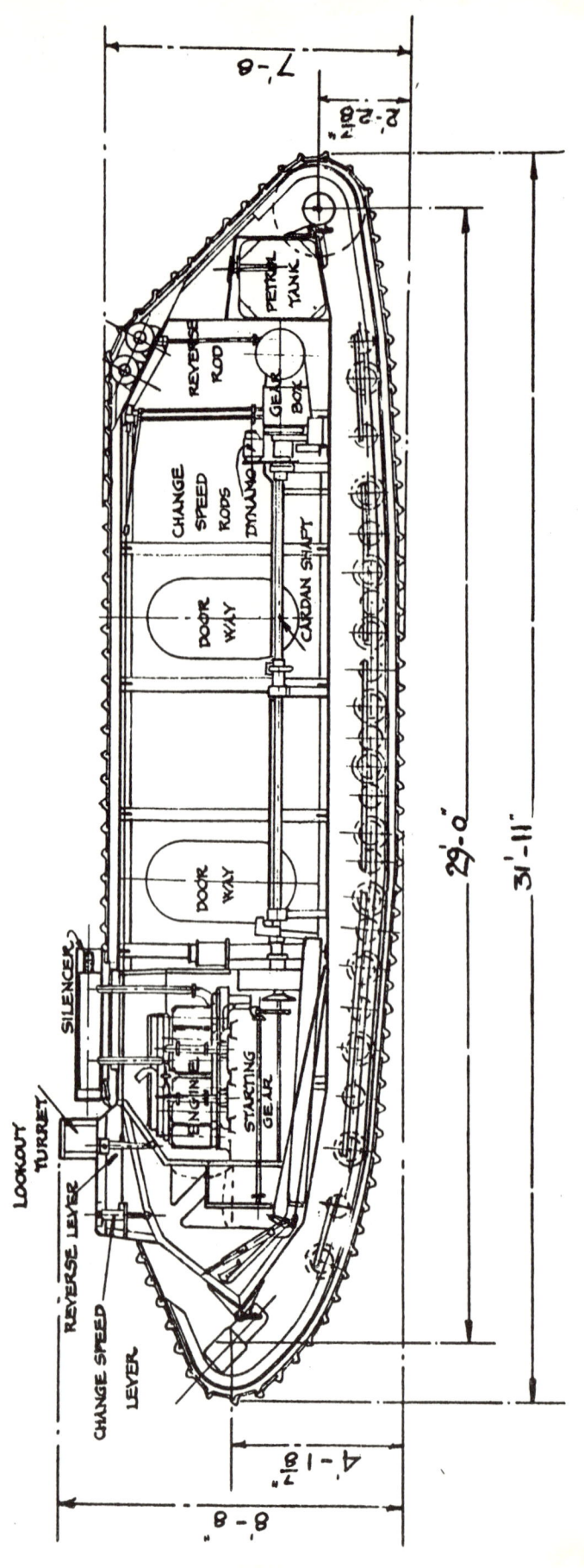

General arrangement of Machine Mark IX

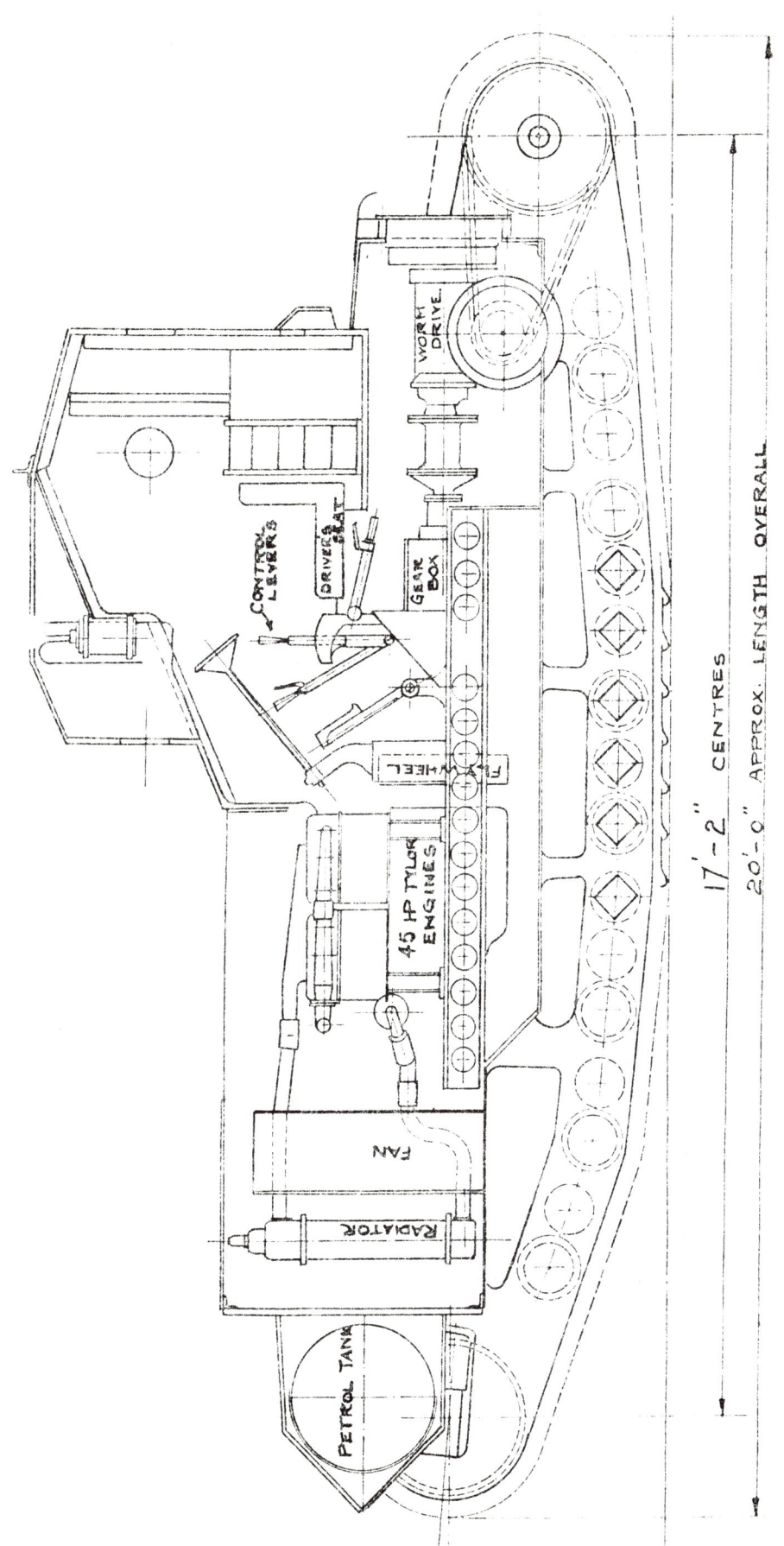

General arrangement of Machine Medium Mark 'A'

General arrangement of Medium Mark 'B'

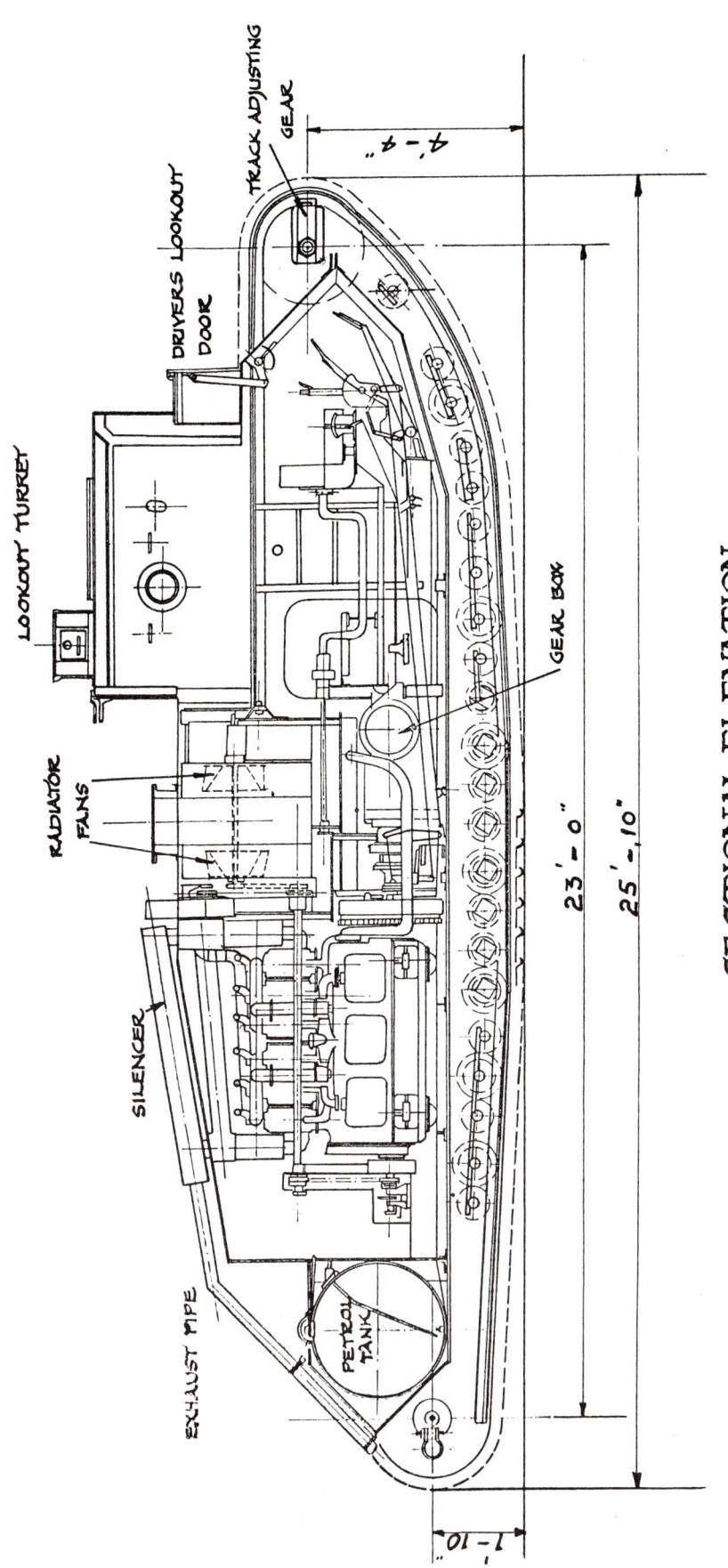

General arrangement of Machine Medium Mark 'C'

Index

Allenby, General Sir Edmund 28
Amiens 36
Army, Australian 24, 34
Army, British
   6th Kings Own Yorkshire Light Infantry 16
   63rd (Royal Naval) Division 17
Army, French 35
Army, United States 31, 34
Arnold, Lieutenant C. B. 36
Arras 24
Austin Armoured Cars 36

Bacon, Admiral Sir Reginald 89
Beaumont-Hamel 17
Bentley, Lieutenant W. O. 26
Bermicourt 17
Big Wheel Machine 5, 8
Bovington Camp 2, 18, 19, 43
Bullecourt 24
Bullock Tractor 7, 10
Burstyn, Gunther 3

Cambrai 28
Churchill, W. S. L. 3, 4, 5, 8, 10, 31, 46
Cowen, James 1
Crompton, Colonel R. E. B. 2, 4, 5, 7, 10, 11, 13, 46

Diplock, Bramah J. 4, 5, 7

Elephant's Feet 10
Elles, Lieut.-Col. Hugh 18, 28, 29, 37
Elveden 14
Erin 18
Experimental Bridging Establishment 14
D'Eyncourt, Eustace T. 4

Flying Elephant 23
Foster-Daimler Tractor 8, 11
Freyberg VC, Colonel C. B. 17
Fuller, Colonel J. F. C. 18, 28, 45

Gaza 24, 28
Gore-Anley, Brigadier General F. 19
Gun Carrier 26

HMS *Excellent* 14
Haig, Field Marshal Sir Douglas 15, 17, 21, 25
Hamel 34
Hankey, Lieut.-Col. Maurice 9
Hatfield Park 13, 14
Hetherington, Commander T. G. 5, 7
Holt Tractor 3, 4, 9
Hotblack, Captain F. E. 25

Hush Operation 26, 45

Johnson, Lieut.-Col. Philip 45, 46

Killen Strait Tractor 7, 10
Kitchener, Lord 13

Landships Committee 2, 4, 10, 11, 12
Legros, L. A. 10, 11, 46
Lincoln 9, 12
Little Willie 12
Lloyd-George, David 10, 13
Lulworth 18

MacFie, Lieut. R. F. 7, 46
Merlimont 18, 26
Messines Ridge 25
Metropolitan Carriage, Wagon & Finance Co. 14
Mitchell, Lieut. Frank 34
de Mole, Lancelot E. 3, 46
Moreuil 35
Mother 13, 14, 22

Number 1 Lincoln Machine 11

Oldbury Trials 22

Pedrail Machine 8
Pedrail Tractor Co. 4
Plan 1919 45
Price, Captain Tommy 34

Ricardo, Harry 31
Richard Hornsby & Sons Ltd 3
Rigby, William 10, 11
Roberts, David 3
Robertson VC, Captain Clement 25
Rollencourt 18
Roller Track Wagon 8
Royal Commission 46

St. Julien 25
Samson, Commander C. R. 1, 3
Sewell VC, Lieut. C. H. 38
Simms, Frederick 1
Solomon, Lieut.-Col. Solomon J. 17
Stern, Albert 2, 6, 10, 11, 12, 21, 31, 41, 46
Sueter, Commodore Murray 4, 5, 7, 10, 14
Swanage 18
Swinton, Colonel Ernest 3, 9, 14, 15

Tadpole Tail 27
Tank Corps 25
Tank Museum 2

Tanks, British Heavy;
   Mark I 14, 24, 38
   Mark II 18, 19, 22, 24
   Mark III 18, 19
   Mark IV 21, 22, 24, 25, 31, 33, 34, 38, 43
   Mark V 31, 34, 35, 40, 42, 45
   Mark V* 35, 40
   Mark V** 40
   Mark VI 31, 41
   Mark VII 40
   Mark VIII 41
   Mark IX 41, 42
Tanks, British Medium;
   Mark A (Whippet) 33, 34, 35, 36, 38, 42
   Mark B 38, 42
   Mark C 38
   Mark D 45
Tanks, German, A7V 33, 34
Tritton Chaser 23, 37
Tritton Trench Crosser 9, 12
Tritton, Sir William 2, 10, 11, 14, 23, 38, 46
20 Squadron RNAS 1, 8, 9, 10, 13, 46

Villers Bretonneux 34

Wailly 18
Wain VC, Captain R. W. C. 30
Wareham 18
West VC, Lieut.-Col. R. A. 38
William Foster & Co. 2, 6, 14, 23
Wilson, Walter G. 2, 6, 7, 11, 12, 13, 14, 21, 22, 38, 46

Ypres, 3rd Battle of 25

Printed in the UK for HMSO
Dd 736189 C30 5/84